NEWBORN CARE MADE EASY

A FIRST TIME MOM'S NO-NONSENSE GUIDE TO NEWBORN EXPECTATIONS, POSTPARTUM RECOVERY, AND BEYOND

Krista Barrack

Copyright © 2023 Krista Barrack

All rights reserved. This publication, or any part thereof, may not be reproduced in any form, or by any means, including electronic, photographic, or mechanical, or by any sound recording system, or by any device for storage and retrieval of information, without the written permission of the copyright owner.

Table of Contents

Introduction 4
Chapter 1: Getting Your Home Ready for a Baby................8
    Baby Proof Your Home for Safety..............................8
    Be Prepared for a Feeding Frenzy............................13
Chapter 2: Must Have Newborn Items................................21
    Baby Clothes...22
    Baby Bathing Supplies..38
    Sick Baby Supplies...39
    Nice to Haves..48
    Setup a Registry!..49
Chapter 3: Parenting as a Team..51
    Practical Tips for Parenting as a Team....................52
    Maternity Leave Doesn't Last Long..........................55
    How to Choose a Daycare...56
    It Takes a Village..57
Chapter 4: Packing for the Hospital/Birth Center............60
Chapter 5: Pregnancy and Birth Complications...............68
    Common Pregnancy Complications........................69
    Risk Factors for Birth Complications.......................72
Chapter 6: Basics of Postpartum Care................................75
    Vaginal Delivery Postpartum Care............................78
    C-Section Recovery..84
Chapter 7: Navigating Your Mental Health.........................88
    Your Self-Care is Essential...89
    An Introduction to Postpartum Depression...........94

Table of Contents

Chapter 8: 0-1 Month Old Baby..97
    Newborn Crying..98
    Newborn Sleep..102
    Feeding..103
    Diapering..105

Chapter 9: 1-2 Month Old Baby..112
    Crying..113
    Sleeping..114
    Feeding..116
    Diapering..118
    Developmental Milestones..120
    Activities..121

Chapter 10: 2-3 Month Old Baby..124
    Crying..125
    Sleeping..126
    Feeding..128
    Diapering..130
    Developmental Milestones..131
    Activities..133

Conclusion Mama, You've Got This..136

Checklists..146

Introduction

Becoming a parent for the first time can be one of your life's most exciting and overwhelming experiences. Suddenly, you are responsible for a tiny human being who is entirely reliant on you to meet their needs and teach them how to thrive in this world. While having a new addition to your family is lovely, it can also be incredibly challenging and stressful.

As a first-time parent, you feel clueless and helpless, especially if you have limited experience caring for other babies. Or you are one of the first of your friends to have a baby, so you feel like you don't have too many people to lean on for help. Trust me; I've been there. Although newborns are challenging, this book empowers first time moms with knowledge on what to expect to make newborn care easier.

One of the things that we hear on repeat is people constantly telling us that parenting is hard. I'm sorry to say I won't be able to tell you otherwise. However, I can share some more context on what is hard so you are not left in the dark.

In addition, throughout this book, we will also be diving into some common things that are important to know as parents, such as feeding habits, sleeping habits, developmental milestones, activities, and more, to help you know you are on the right track with this new parenting experience.

Let's first talk about the emotional challenges of becoming a parent. When you become a first-time parent, you will face a wide range of emotions ranging from joy, happiness, and excitement to fear, anxiety, and exhaustion. On the one hand, you'll feel immense love and pride for your child, which are lovely feelings! On the other hand, there will be times when you feel overwhelmed by the responsibility that comes with parenting. It is normal to experience all these emotions as you transition into this new role; however, managing them all at once can still be challenging.

Financial challenges will also arise, and first-time parents often feel the financial strain. Having children significantly changes your budget—you may need to purchase baby supplies such as diapers and formula or larger items like strollers or car seats. In addition, childcare costs can add up quickly if both parents work or one parent decides to stay home with the baby full-time. Therefore, planning ahead financially before having children is essential so that you are better prepared for these expenses.

On top of the complex emotional challenges and financial strain, let's not forget about sleep deprivation. Sleep deprivation is one of the most common issues new parents (especially mothers) face.

With so much on their plate, including changing diapers, feeding babies, and dealing with constant crying, it can be hard for parents to get their much-needed rest. Lack of sleep can severely affect mental and physical health, so new parents need to ensure they're getting enough rest when possible. To combat sleep deprivation, try to set aside time daily for yourself and your partner to relax and recharge; even just 20 minutes can make a big difference! Also, don't hesitate to ask family members or friends for help when needed. This will give you more time to catch up on sleep or relax after a long day.

Managing your time will also be something new you have to navigate differently. You might be exhausted from late nights spent caring for your baby or struggling to balance work and parenting responsibilities. This lack of "me-time" can make it difficult to maintain relationships outside of parenthood or focus on other tasks such as work or housework.

Before you are thrown into this new experience, the biggest advice I can offer is not to have too many expectations. Most new parents have certain expectations about what parenting looks like before they actually become parents themselves. However, these expectations often don't match reality, leading to frustration and disappointment when things don't go as planned. To avoid this issue, try not to have too many expectations about how things should be; instead, focus on being flexible and adaptable when things don't go according to plan (which they likely won't!). Additionally, remember that becoming a parent isn't easy—so cut yourself some slack if things aren't going as smoothly as you had hoped!

Though it may be hard to believe during early morning feedings and never-ending diaper changes, things will eventually get easier. With some help and guidance, you'll be able to navigate this new landscape like a pro. You are already on the right path by continuing to read this book on newborn care basics; it covers everything from feedings to sleep expectations (and beyond).

Congratulations again on expecting your new arrival – parenthood is a fantastic journey! Be sure to stock up on diapers, formula, and this book so you'll be as prepared as possible for everything ahead.

Chapter 1
Getting Your Home Ready for A Baby

Bringing a newborn home is an exciting time for any family. But before the baby arrives, it's important to ensure your home is ready to welcome the little bundle of joy. From ensuring that your nursery is set up to stocking up on essential supplies, there are many steps you should take to ensure your home is safe and comfortable for you and your baby.

Baby Proof Your Home for Safety

Safety is the most important thing when preparing your home for a newborn. Unfortunately, many parents believe they can skip this step early and just wait until the baby is more mobile. I learned from that mistake, so I am telling you to get on it early. The problem with waiting until they are more mobile is that you are already doing what feels like 100 things a day, then having to worry about baby-proofing at that point just adds to the exhaustion. Don't do that; get a jump start on it now.

Start by going around your house and ensuring that all potential hazards are removed (or made inaccessible). Baby-proofing your home is crucial for any parent or guardian wanting to ensure their child's safety. Making sure that tiny, unsafe objects are out of reach, harmful chemicals are locked away, and all electrical outlets are covered is vital in keeping children safe and healthy.

For example, now that my little man is on the move, he yanks on the kitchen cabinets, which are locked up. However, we never baby-proofed the cabinets in the bathroom. So now he enjoys digging through my nail polish boxes and pulling all my period pads from their packaging. Again learn from me and put locks on the kitchen and bathroom cabinets.

Many injuries can be avoided by baby-proofing; everything from skid-proofing floors to securing furniture needs to be considered. It's not just about physical safety; parental supervision is also essential to ensure children aren't accessing things they shouldn't be. Baby-proofing your home may seem like an arduous task, but it can go a long way towards understanding the needs of a child and giving them a happy, protective environment to explore.

This includes putting away sharp or breakable things and potential choking hazards, such as small objects or long strings/cords. Get rid of any toxic chemicals or cleaners, and secure all furniture and appliances with childproof locks. Finally, install smoke alarms in every room and check them regularly.

Creating A Safe Sleeping Space

A newborn needs a safe sleeping space to ensure health and well-being. Therefore, it is important to provide them with a sleep environment that will be conducive to quality rest and free from potential hazards that could result in harm. Creating an optimum sleeping area for your infant helps minimize the risk of SIDS and gives you peace of mind that they are getting the best sleep they can while keeping them safe. Appropriate bedding and clothing should be used, along with a cleared-out space, free from clutter or other items that may present a danger.

The crib should also meet proper mattress construction and fit guidelines to reduce any potential risks associated with incorrect use. Providing a secure slumber area for your baby can help ensure their safety and foster an atmosphere conducive to healthy development. You should avoid having your baby sleep on couches, waterbeds, armchairs, or anywhere else that isn't specifically designed for babies to sleep. Additionally, having your child sleep in a car seat, swing, infant nest, or other unapproved sleeping items is not recommended.

Although, from mama to mama, I definitely was not perfect at following all the guidelines. Sometimes you are just in survival mode, and I one hundred percent understand that. Just keep doing the best you can and making the safest decisions you can for your children.

What is SIDS?

Sudden Infant Death Syndrome, or SIDS, is an unexplained death of a seemingly healthy infant. It is characterized by the abrupt and unexpected death of an infant before the age of 1 year old with no known cause. Although it is not completely preventable, understanding the risk factors for SIDS can help ensure that infants sleep safely.

Breastfeeding, immunizations, avoiding smoke exposure during and after pregnancy, sleeping babies on their backs, and using a firm crib mattress can all help reduce risks. Additionally, keeping a baby's sleeping area free from bulky blankets or stuffed animals can help reduce risk and avoid overly hot or cold temperatures when putting a baby to bed. Recognizing SIDS is an important part of providing safe care for infants and understanding the risk factors may reduce its occurrence.

Crib or Bassinet?

One of the first decisions a new parent must make is where their newborn should sleep at night. However, deciding between a crib and a bassinet can be difficult. Both provide their own advantages and features that should be considered when making this important family decision. Cribs are typically larger and can hold your little one until they reach three or four years old, whereas bassinets offer improved mobility for parents. Unfortunately, my little monkey could crawl out of the crib before 18 months old. However, that didn't matter much because we ended up co-sleeping anyway.

One benefit of using a bassinet over a crib is that you can easily rock a baby to sleep in a bassinet without getting up from bed. Additionally, many come with wheels that allow you to move them around the home or outside more conveniently than a crib. Another benefit is that some consider changing their baby's diaper in a bassinet's confinements faster and easier than in a big bulky crib. However, safety is still the number one priority, so that should always be considered throughout this process.

Some parents even opt for a pack-and-play for their newborn to sleep in because they are versatile and can help save the parents money by not having to buy as many products. Ultimately, the sleeping option is up to you. Because this was my first child, I was eager to set up a nursery with a crib, but I also had a pack-and-play and a rocking bassinet. I will say that I became a big fan of the 4Moms rocking bassinet. It did help soothe my son to sleep because he loved the motion.

More on Sleeping Space Safety

Some of this information may seem trivial, but providing a safe sleeping environment for a baby, especially a newborn, is critical. When setting up a safe sleeping space for your newborn, it is important to ensure that all furniture and bedding are up-to-date and meet safety standards. Make sure any cribs or bassinets have passed safety tests and are free from hazards such as loose screws or sharp edges.

We sometimes prefer to buy used stuff from Facebook Market or Craigslist to save money, but when it comes to baby items, it is ideal to buy new so that you have the owner's handbook and know it is safely put together with all the necessary parts.

Once you've put your crib or bassinet together, it's also important to ensure the mattress fits snugly into the crib frame. Make sure there aren't any gaps where your baby could become stuck or smothered. When choosing bedding, select light sheets that won't overheat your baby; you should also avoid using pillows, crib bumpers, or stuffed animals in the crib.

Basic Baby Sleeping Supplies:

- Crib, bassinet, or pack n' play
- An appropriate fitting mattress for the sleeping space
- Several fitted sheets (baby may soil sheets, so it's best to be prepared)

Be Prepared for A Feeding Frenzy

It is important to remember that newborn babies must be fed often and require frequent nourishment. In their first few weeks, they will need up to twelve feedings daily, with some even needing to eat every few hours. Newborns frequently eat as their little tummies can only hold a small amount of milk or formula at once. To make sure your baby is properly nourished, you need to be prepared ahead of time with bottles, nipples, and any other necessary materials to meet their nutritional needs.

Being adequately prepared for feeding sessions can help make the experience more manageable for both baby and caregiver, from having sufficient bottles on hand to

stocking cupboards with necessary groceries. In addition, by preparing ahead of time, parents and caretakers can ensure that the precious moments spent nourishing a little one are comfortable and safe for everyone involved.
I remember having a feeding schedule that I would try to follow like clockwork. I was one of the crazy moms who would wake the baby to feed him. But that wasn't always necessary because ==one neat trick about newborns is that they can eat and sleep at the same time. Imagine that!==

Breastfeeding or Formula Feeding?

Expecting mothers who know they intend to breastfeed their newborn should still plan to have a backup formula feeding plan in case of any complications. While breastfeeding is generally considered the healthiest option for both mother and baby, there may be times when a newborn must be formula-fed due to unforeseen circumstances, such as if the mother's milk does not come in on time or if the baby is born prematurely. For these reasons, it is important to always be prepared with a reliable formula, just in case. Being informed and having everything ready can help ease stress and worry if any future breastfeeding issues arise.

If breastfeeding is not your choice, and you prefer formula feeding, that's also a great option. As an alternative to breastfeeding, formula feeding can provide many advantages, such as parents having more freedom and flexibility with feeding schedules, the ability to share feeding duties with different family members, more insight into the quantity of formula consumed by babies, and no nutritional restrictions.

It is important to note that formula feeding is not inferior to breastfeeding; it can be just as effective when used according to your healthcare provider's guidelines. Formula feeding has unique benefits, allowing parents to provide the best nutrition possible for their little ones.

As I mentioned earlier, not to have too many expectations, this again is a piece of advice I learned along the way with motherhood. I thought breastfeeding would come easily or naturally, but I struggled with it. My son had difficulty latching, and I had an easier time just getting him to take milk from a bottle. So whatever is your feeding story, do what works best for you and your child. Just remember, you got this, mama. Take one step at a time!

Breastfeeding Guidelines

Breastfeeding is one of the best ways to nourish and nurture your newborn. It is also recommended by many health organizations, such as the World Health Organization, that mothers exclusively breastfeed for the first six months after birth. Afterward, it is recommended to continue to breastfeed (in combination with other foods) until the baby is at least one year old.

Breastfeeding strengthens the bond between mother and baby and provides essential nutrients for proper growth, development, and long-term health benefits for both mother and baby. In order to establish a successful breastfeeding experience for you and your baby, there are some important guidelines to keep in mind: feed on demand; ensure adequate sleep; avoid pacifiers; dress comfortably; maintain good posture; eat nutritious food;

drink plenty of fluids; seek advice from experienced healthcare professionals; and find support amongst family members or other nursing mothers.

Breast Milk Storage Tips

- When storing breast milk, label the container with a date. *and time - night time has melatonin*
- Don't store breast milk in the door of the fridge or freezer.
- Freeze breast milk in small containers of 4oz to avoid waste.
- Breast milk can be stored at room temperate for up to 4 hours.
- Breast milk can be stored in the refrigerator for up to 4 days.
- Breast milk can be frozen for up to one year.

Breastfeeding Supplies

- Breast pump (many are covered by insurance, so don't forget to check)

> **NOTE**
>
> In my own experience, I felt like the hands-free ones made a huge difference, as you could pump and hold your baby and walk around simultaneously. Hands-free technology brings a lot of conveniences.

Breastfeeding Supplies
- Breast pump parts

> **NOTE**
>
> I wanted to provide some context on this because my personal breastfeeding journey was cut short by my lack of education at the time. Breast pumps have flanges of different sizes; Using the wrong size flange may impact your milk supply. Try to stock up on different sizes in advance to see what best works for you, or get a fitting from a consultant.

- Breast milk storage bags
- Nipple Cream
- Nursing Bras
- Nursing Pads
- Baby bottles
- Slow-flow nipples for the bottles
- Burb cloths
- Bottlebrush

Formula Feeding Guidelines

Preparing and storing infant formula correctly is essential to ensuring that your baby receives the necessary nutrients for healthy growth. Before feeding, the formula should be thoroughly mixed with boiled and cooled water according to the ratio listed on the label.

Pre-made formula products do not require additional preparation. Make sure you only use the scoop from the packaging - level it off using a knife or other flat object afterward. Discard any leftover formula after feeding to prevent bacteria growth. If it can be stored, keep it refrigerated for no longer than 24 hours and discard it afterward. It is also important to remember to always use clean bottles and nipples when giving your baby their liquid gold!

Formula Feeding Supplies

- Formula

> **NOTE**
>
> Choosing a formula is up to you, but you may want to have a few on hand in case the baby does not react well to just one kind. Usually, you can obtain samples from the manufacturer, which typically provides you with several options.

- Baby bottles
- Slow flow nipples
- Bottle warmer
- Burp cloths
- Bottle brush

Quick Formula Feeding Tips

- Prepared formula can be left out at room temperature for up to 2 hours.
- Prepared formula is only suitable for 1 houronce the baby starts drinking.
- Prepared formula can be stored in the refrigerator for up to 24 hours.
- Store your formula container in a cool, dry place, not the refrigerator.
- Once a formula container is opened, it should be used within 1 month.
- Never use the formula after the use-by date; it has expired.

While I always did my best to follow the guidelines and formula feeding tips, I tried not to let myself stress too much. I know some moms out there would immediately set a timer and dump the milk even before the one hour expired. I found that to be fairly stressful, so I just winged it for the most part. Just remember to keep doing the best you can, mama. No judgment here!

Should you sterilize baby bottles?

It is essential to sterilize baby bottles for newborns, as it can help protect your infant's health. By sterilizing bottles regularly, you can remove and reduce the presence of harmful bacteria that could otherwise affect your baby's health. As such, it is essential to ensure that baby bottles are adequately cleaned and sterilized with boiling water or a steam-based appliance before each feed. This will aid in providing all the necessary nutrients while protecting against sickness and infection, which can be especially detrimental during an infant's early life stages. Thus, it is advised to ensure that baby bottles undergo regular cleansing and sterilization for your baby's safety and healthy growth.

Today, many dishwashers have sanitizing options, but they tend to extend the cycle considerably. If you are looking for a quick and easy way to properly sterilize bottles, I would suggest just looking for a bottle sterilizer on Amazon.

Chapter 2
Must Have Newborn Items

When bringing a new baby home, knowing exactly what you need can be hard. First, having the correct type of car seat is essential for safely and legally transporting your bundle of joy. Beyond that, some items that every expecting parent should have on hand is a changing table (or somewhere convenient to change baby's diapers), a crib or bassinet for sleeping, and a few receiving blankets.

Another important item is clothing; onesies, sleepers, and socks should be available in the correct size for when the baby arrives. Additional important items would include bath time essentials. A plastic tub with support and at least five hooded towels and washcloths are necessary for bath time. Lastly, a diaper bag will be handy for nursing items, diapers, and other disposable products like wipes, among many other things – but just make sure it's roomy enough to last several hours away from home!

Baby Clothes

As much as parents love shopping for cute outfits for their babies, it's important to remember that babies grow quickly in their first few months. Therefore, it's best to shop strategically by purchasing quality basics like onesies, sleepers, socks, and hats in sizes up to three months ahead of time. This will help ensure your baby has enough clothing while growing rapidly. It is also important to note that babies can be quite messy, so having plenty of extra clothes on hand is always helpful!

Many people advised me to avoid buying "newborn" sizes because babies grow so fast. However, in my case, that backfired. My baby boy was born at only 6lbs, so he was just itty bitty, and the 0-3 month clothes were just too bulky on him. So I think it is a good idea to still make sure you pick up a few things in newborn sizes as you never know what size baby you are going to get.

How much clothing should you buy for a newborn?

When it comes to how much clothing you should buy for your newborn, the answer really depends on your lifestyle. Purchasing multiple outfits is a good idea if you plan to change the baby's outfit often. Also, think about how much time you will have to do laundry. There are enough things to do when suddenly caring for a newborn that you may not have time for that. You may have to change your baby more frequently than you think between blow-outs and spit-ups. This is why it's always a good idea to stock up but not overstock.

However, if you prefer dressing them in fewer but higher quality pieces, investing in a few quality items that can be worn in multiple settings may be a better choice. Remember that babies grow quickly, and they will outgrow their clothes before you know it! Shopping secondhand can also be a great way to get more bang for your buck while ensuring your bundle of joy has the best of the best.

Here are some recommendations to help you know how much to buy.

Baby Clothes to Buy...

- Onesies
    - Onesies in newborn size
    - Onesies in 0-3 months size
- Long Sleeve Body Suit
    - Fall/Winter Baby
        - 5 in newborn size
        - 10 in 0-3 month size
    - Spring/Summer Baby
        - 3 in newborn size
        - 5 in 0-3 month size
- Pants
    - 3 Pants in newborn size
    - 5 Pants in 0-3 months size
- Footie Pajamas
    - 5 in newborn size
    - 10 in 0-3 months size

> **NOTE**
> I think the footie PJs were the easiest to work with in the newborn stages. Also, as a pro tip, avoid the snap-up style and just go with the zip-up kind. They may be a little more expensive, but they are a huge convenience!

- Hats and Mittens
    - 3 Hats
    - 5 Mittens
- Socks
    - 12 pairs of 0-3 months size
- Outerwear
    - Fall/Winter Baby
        - 1 Coat or bunting outfit
        - 2 Sweaters or Hoodies
- Swaddles
    - 3-4 Swaddles
- Blankets
    - 2 Baby blankets

CHECKlist — SEE THE FULL CHECKLIST AT THE BACK OF THE BOOK TO MAKE SURE YOU ARE NOT MISSING ANY NEWBORN MUST HAVE ITEMS!

A Car Seat is a Must Have

When traveling by car, having an appropriate car seat for a newborn is essential for their safety. Although taking an infant anywhere in a car can be intimidating, following car seat laws and regulations installed for their protection will help put parents' minds at ease.

Car seats provide the extra support infants need with their still-developing body structures and reduce the risk of injury in the event of an accident. Also, car seats are designed to be used from birth until at least age 4 or 5, depending on the model, making them a long-term solution.

Parents must use the right size and kind of car seat that suits their child's age and height according to the manufacturer's instructions to ensure maximum safety and security for babies in vehicles.

What to Look for When Buying a Car Seat

When shopping for a car seat for a newborn, there are several factors to consider. First, it should have an appropriate weight and height limit that fits your baby's current size and allows for growth. The seat should also be installed correctly in the backseat of your vehicle per the instructions to ensure optimum safety.

Additionally, look for an adjustable car seat to allow you to adjust the harness straps and headrest as your child grows. You should also check that it has crash-tested certification from an agency such as NHTSA or IIHS, ensuring it meets safety standards and will give your child maximum protection in case of an accident. Lastly, try to find one with a comfortable padded cushion if possible — not just on the newborn insert but on the body of the car seat; it'll make long rides more pleasant for everyone!

Convertible Car Seat vs. Infant Car Seat

Many safety decisions must be made when welcoming a new baby into the world. One of the most important is which car seat to purchase for your little one. There are many different types of car seats, but the two most common are infant car seats and convertible car seats. This section will explore both types and discuss the best for a newborn.

Infant Car Seats:

An infant car seat is designed specifically for newborns or infants (weighing up to 30 pounds). The advantage of this type of seat is that it provides extra support and cushioning for tiny babies who still need additional protection while on the road. Additionally, they are lightweight and moveable from one vehicle to another, making them great for those who use multiple vehicles or often travel with their babies.

Another advantage of an infant seat is that you can easily attach them to a stroller. Typically you can find package deals called travel systems that come with an infant car seat and a stroller. This means that if your baby falls asleep in the car while you are on the go, you can quickly transfer them to the stroller and be on your way without waking them.

The disadvantage of an infant car seat is that your baby will quickly outgrow an infant car seat (usually around 12 months) and will need a new one once they reach 30 pounds or more. This can become costly over time if you have multiple children who require new seats every year or so.

Personally, I opted for the infant car seat that snapped to my stroller. It was a lot easier to load the baby into the seat in the house, which was nice and warm in the winter, and just snap it into the base of the car. But, around my son's first birthday, I realized I needed to upgrade to a convertible car seat to offer him more room to grow.

Convertible Car Seats:

A convertible car seat is designed to grow with your child from infancy all the way up to toddlerhood. It can be used as a rear-facing seat for babies weighing 5-40 pounds, then converted into a forward-facing seat for toddlers weighing up to 65 pounds. Convertible car seats also come with adjustable headrests and side impact protection to keep your baby safe even during unexpected stops or crashes. Additionally, they often come with more features like cup holders and snack trays, and there are even some on the market with built-in speakers so your child stays entertained while traveling in their seat.

The advantage of this type of seat is that it does not need to be replaced as your child grows, which means you don't have to buy multiple seats over time. However, some parents may find it difficult to install a convertible car seat correctly due to its size and weight. Additionally, it may not fit well in smaller cars or if multiple passengers are in the backseat due to its larger size.

Avoid Buying a Used Car Seat

There are many good reasons for wanting to buy a used car seat. It could be that you're on a tight budget, or you plan to use the car seat briefly before your little one outgrows it. But no matter the reason, buying a used car seat is not recommended, and here's why.

1. Car Seat Safety Standards Change Over Time

Car seats undergo safety tests for particular models every 3-5 years, and sometimes these tests result in safety design changes. If you buy a used car seat, it may not have been tested according to current standards. It could have been recalled, or it could be missing components that would make it safer to use. Furthermore, some manufacturers stop making spare parts for older models, so if parts need replacing, you won't be able to get them from the manufacturer.

2. There Could be Hidden Damage

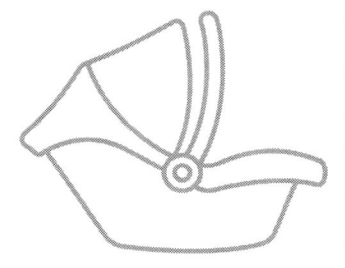

Used car seats can also have hidden damage that isn't apparent at first glance. For instance, even though the fabric looks clean and intact, unseen tears could weaken its strength and compromise its safety.

Likewise, if the car seat has been involved in an accident—even just a minor fender-bender—it may have sustained damage that affects its integrity and puts your child at risk of injury during an accident.

3. Potential Recalls You Don't Know About

Car seat safety standards constantly evolve as engineers learn more about what works best for keeping children safe in cars. Unfortunately, that means that older models may not meet current safety standards or may have been recalled due to safety issues that were discovered after their initial sale date. Manufacturers usually send out notices about recalls, but if you purchase a used car seat, you may not receive these notifications or be able to return the item for repairs or a replacement like you would with a new one.

4. It's History

Finally, when you buy a used car seat, you need to know how many hands it has passed through or how well it was cared for by previous owners. They may have read all the instructions before using the product if they followed all the required steps or if they stored and transported the car seat properly over time. All these things can affect your child's safety when using the product. Since you don't know the history of usage of the product, buying used is risky business!

When it comes to your child's safety while traveling in a vehicle, there should always be room for compromise. This is why buying used is not recommended when shopping for baby products like car seats. To ensure your child's optimal safety while riding in cars, always use brand-new products that are up-to-date with current safety standards and come with fresh warranties in case something goes wrong down the line.

This way, you can rest assured that your precious cargo will travel safely and soundly!

If you want a good deal on a big purchase, watch out for sales around holidays; usually, a good promotion is going on. Also, if you are an Amazon shopper, I've noticed several car-seat deals coming up during Amazon prime day, so don't forget to set a reminder. Another place where you can buy good big-ticket brand-name baby items at usually around 20% off is Albee Baby, an online retailer.

A Stroller

For parents with a newborn baby, strollers can be an invaluable tool for providing comfort and convenience. With their adjustable handles, most strollers can easily maneuver in tight spaces. Many models also have multiple recline positions that can be used to accommodate sleeping babies comfortably.

Some higher-end models even include swivel suspension wheels, allowing parents to effortlessly glide over rough terrains like gravel or unpaved streets. The storage basket beneath the seat is conveniently useful for carrying diapers, wipes, bottles, and other essentials for on-the-go needs. This can help make traveling with a newborn baby much easier and less overwhelming for parents.

Another benefit is that if you are gifted or have already purchased an infant car seat but have yet to purchase a stroller, you can look for a stroller that is compatible with your infant seat. Many strollers have adapters to connect to other brands of infant car seats, but those adapters are mostly sold separately. If you still need to purchase a stroller or a car seat, look for a travel system that combines a stroller and a car seat, as this can help you save money.

Choosing a compatible stroller for your infant car seat is an important decision because it allows you to use the same car seat in different settings without having to move your baby in and out of different seats. This can be particularly helpful if your baby falls asleep in the car seat, as you can simply move the car seat onto the stroller without waking them up.

When choosing a stroller, you'll want to consider its size, weight, and features, such as the number of wheels, the type of suspension, and the folding mechanism. For example, a lightweight stroller may be easier to maneuver, but it may not be as sturdy as a heavier one. Likewise, a stroller with four wheels may provide more stability than a three-wheeled stroller, but it may not be as maneuverable. One popular stroller that you will often see mom-influencers use is called the Doona.

The Doona, a hybrid between a stroller and an infant car seat, is currently a highly popular stroller. The Doona stroller provides parents with a multifunctional and convenient option for transporting their babies and toddlers. After unfolding the stroller, it instantly turns into a car seat with a five-point safety harness, creating an all-in-one product.

Its lightweight design makes it easy to lift, maneuver, and store away without needing to buy additional components.

The Doona also offers great suspension, allowing for comfortable rides for both baby and parent. The individually adjustable handlebar creates even more comfort for the parent or caretaker to push the stroller. Another advantage, and something unique to this stroller, is that its car safety certification tests have been completed according to industry standards from all around the world, meaning parents can feel confident that their children are receiving optimal protection while utilizing the Doona stroller.

Of course, you don't have to buy a Doona stroller, there are plenty of options on the market, and it's easy to get overwhelmed with what to buy. Make sure you check out buying guides and read as many reviews as possible before making your purchase because these are big-ticket items you want to last.

Another point to consider is that if you plan to have multiple children close in age, it would be wise to invest in a stroller that can accommodate more than one child. An expandable stroller is an ideal choice for parents who want to save money and space, as it can convert from a single to a double or even a triple stroller. This type of stroller can accommodate multiple children of different ages and sizes, and it can be easily adjusted to fit your family's changing needs.

An expandable stroller offers several advantages over traditional strollers, including greater flexibility and versatility. With an expandable stroller, you can easily transport two or more children at once, which is particularly useful if you have twins or multiple young children.

Additionally, an expandable stroller can be used for many years, making it a smart long-term investment. Overall, if you are planning to have multiple children close in age, an expandable stroller is an excellent option that will provide you with the flexibility and convenience you need to keep your family moving.

Diapers

Newborn babies often require many diaper changes daily, and it is no surprise that their parents go through many diapers. This can be a daunting task for those taking care of infants, but there are some strategies to make changing diapers easier. Using cloth and disposable diapers can help keep costs down while allowing parents to respond quickly to messes, as they can simply dispose of soiled disposable ones while reusing cloth when needed.

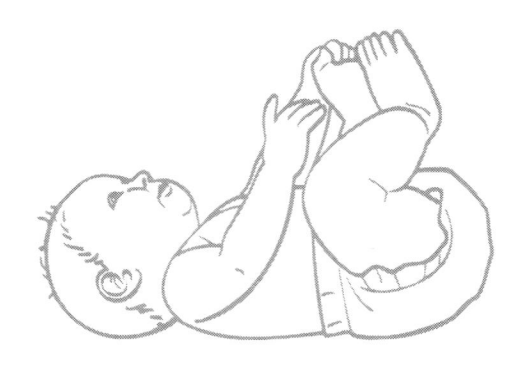

Pre-folded cloth diapers are convenient and easy to use, and with modern materials, they are more absorbent and comfortable than ever before. Furthermore, choosing the right diaper size is paramount; newborns often need tiny sizes, so be sure that the diapering needs match the baby's age for maximum comfort.

Should You Use Cloth Diapers or Disposable Diapers?

For parents-to-be, deciding between cloth diapers and disposable diapers can be difficult. Both have their pros and cons, and the right option will depend on individual needs. So let's break down the differences between cloth and disposable diapers to help make your decision easier.

Cloth Diapers

Cloth diapers are made of cotton, hemp, or other absorbent materials that must be washed after each use. The material is folded around the baby's bottom and secured with pins or Velcro fasteners. Cloth diapers come in many different styles like pre-folds, contours, all-in-ones, pocket diapers, and fitted. Each type has its unique benefits depending on what you're looking for in a diaper system.

One of the most significant advantages of using cloth diapers is that they're reusable and can be washed repeatedly for multiple uses before replacing them. They also reduce waste because there is no need to throw out used disposables daily. Additionally, many parents find that cloth diapers are more comfortable for their babies than disposables because they provide better air circulation, which helps keep babies cool and dry during use. Some parents also prefer cloth because it gives them more freedom when selecting colors and patterns than disposable brands with limited design options.

On the other hand, there are several downsides to using cloth diapers, including the need to clean them after each use (which can be quite time-consuming), the risk of leaks if not used properly, and the need for frequent diaper changes since they don't absorb moisture as well as disposables do. Moreover, if you have a busy lifestyle, it might not be practical to always use cloth diapers since they require constant tending and washing.

Disposable Diapers

Disposable diapers are designed to be used once before being thrown away in a trash can or diaper pail after use. They are typically made of plastic or synthetic fabric with an absorbent material that absorbs moisture away from the baby's skin into a separate layer, preventing it from leaking out onto clothing or bedding. Disposable diapers come in various sizes, so you can find the best fit possible for your baby, making them convenient since you don't have to worry about folding them correctly, like with cloth diapers.

The convenience factor is huge when it comes to disposable diapers; all you have to do is take off the dirty diaper and put on a new one without worrying about washing or drying anything in between usage! Additionally, some parents find that disposables offer better protection against leaks since they are made with materials specifically designed for this purpose, whereas cloth requires more adjustment time if you want extra protection against leaks (like adding additional layers).Finally, if you often travel with your baby, disposables may be the better option since they don't require any special packing considerations that cloth does (i.e., packing extra clean ones just in case!).

However, there are also several drawbacks associated with disposable diapers, such as their cost. Depending on how often you buy them, they can become quite expensive over time compared to cloth options that you can reuse repeatedly. Additionally, some people worry about health concerns associated with ingredients found in some disposable diaper brands, such as dyes or fragrances, which may cause skin irritation or allergies depending on your baby's individual needs.

Disposable Diaper Sizes for Most Newborns

- Size P1 Diapers - Babies Less than 6lbs
- Newborn Diapers - Babies Up to 10lbs
- Size 1 Diapers - Babies 8-14lbs
- Size 2 Diapers - Babies 12-18lbs

Additional diaper buying tips...

When it comes to buying diapers, there are many factors to consider. First, determine the size and number of diapers you need depending on your baby's age, size, and activity level. Next, look for labels that indicate hypoallergenic materials or natural cotton content if your baby has sensitive skin or allergies. When selecting a particular diaper brand, you should also factor in absorption level, leg fit, and sturdiness. Finally, buy bigger packages of diapers since those tend to be more cost-efficient than smaller bundles. When done right, these tips can help make diaper shopping easier and more economical for everyone.

Diaper Rash Cream

Diaper rash cream is important in a baby's skincare routine, particularly for those prone to skin irritation. It heals existing diaper rash and prevents new ones from growing by forming a protective layer between the baby's skin and the wet diaper.

Selecting an appropriate product free from fragrances and dyes is crucial as these can further irritate the delicate baby's skin. Additionally, frequent changes of diapers can keep rashes at bay and reduce their occurrence.

Diaper rash creams provide relief and help soothe your baby's bottom while reducing redness and inflammation. Allowing your baby to go without a diaper also helps minimize the chances of diaper rashes. Because diaper rash cream is essential, stock up now, or add it to your Amazon subscription to have it sent to you automatically.

Baby Bathing Supplies

Newborn babies require special care, and a baby bathtub is one of the most essential items. It is important to choose the right type of tub that helps make bath time a safe experience for your little one. A baby bathtub is designed with slip-free material on its bottom, which prevents your baby from slipping or sliding while you are bathing them.

Since newborns are much more delicate than older babies, the removable sling in some of these tubs can provide extra support and comfort during their time in the water. Many baby bathtubs also have sections for sitting and reclining to accommodate different developmental stages, so you will use them for more extended periods. This makes life easier for parents who don't want to worry about buying multiple tubs as their baby grows!

In addition to a baby bathtub, consider adding the following items to your shopping cart.

- Baby body wash
- Baby shampoo
- Baby washcloths
- Baby towels

Sick Baby Supplies

While bringing a new baby into the world is an incredibly joyous occasion, it can also be extremely stressful if the newborn falls ill. Fortunately, there are steps you can take to make sure your little one gets the care they need while at home. Here are some great things to have in case your little one gets ill.

Rectal Thermometer

A rectal thermometer is the most reliable thermometer for a newborn because it measures the core temperature at the source. When it comes to babies, accuracy is paramount. Oral and tympanic ear thermometer readings may differ from rectal readings due to activity levels, eating or drinking before taking the temperature, ambient room and body temperature changes, and other factors that could produce false readings. These discrepancies cannot be afforded when dealing with newborns.

A rectal thermometer also yields an instantaneous reading compared to an electronic tympanic ear thermometer, which can take several minutes before a reading returns, leaving you unsure of the baby's true temperature. Finally, rectal temperatures remain accurate when taken properly for areas where oral or tympanic ear measurements are not possible due to age or physical obstructions.

Infant Pain Reliever

Infant pain relievers, such as Tylenol and Motrin, can be an invaluable resource for parents who want to ensure their child is comfortable and happy. The ability to quickly reduce fever pains or teething aches can greatly reduce stress for both the infant and the parents. Additionally, when used appropriately and according to directions, these products provide safe, effective relief that can make a child feel better quickly.

Having infant pain relievers available gives parents peace of mind knowing they have a tool at their disposal to treat their little one's discomfort. Dosage instructions are printed on the packaging. However, for newborns, you should consult your pediatrician to get the proper amount for the age and weight of your infant.

Snot Sucker / Nasal Aspirator

When welcoming a newborn into the home, having a snot sucker is important. Keeping their nasal passages clear of mucus can make a big difference in their comfort, helping them sleep better and breathe more easily. This device is excellent for removing excess mucus from congested noses, reducing inflammation, and allowing them to make feeding more easily.

It's also a safe way for parents to remove sticky substances that may block their babies' airways without inserting their fingers or any other object. Of course, parents should always consult their pediatrician before using a snot sucker with their newborn, as some healthcare providers may advise against its use. Ultimately, though, having this item readily available can save much unease and provide peace of mind.

Humidifier

A humidifier is often invaluable for helping a sick baby feel more comfortable. The additional humidity helps the mucous membranes of the nose and throat, preventing them from drying out due to fever or allergies. This helps keep their airways lubricated, which helps them cough and sneeze to rid the body of infectious bacteria or viruses.

Another benefit of using a humidifier is that it can help ease dry skin associated with respiratory illness. By adding moisture to the air, it also hydrates their skin, keeping them more comfortable during recovery. Additionally, some parents have noticed that noise from a running humidifier helps soothe their babies back to sleep when they have difficulty sleeping due to nasal congestion or teething.

Saline Spray

A saline spray can help clean your baby's nasal passages and relieve a sick or congested infant. Saline solutions are made up of salt and water, which are both natural ingredients that are safe for your baby's delicate nose. The saline helps to moisturize and loosen built-up mucus in the nasal passages, allowing it to flow more freely and making your baby more comfortable as they recover.

By helping to clear out the sinuses, the saline spray can also alleviate coughing and wheezing symptoms in a baby suffering from congestion due to allergies or a respiratory illness. It not only relieves symptoms, but its moisturizing function may even prevent congestion from occurring in the first place if applied frequently.

Petroleum Jelly

Petroleum jelly has long been a staple for many parents raising infants. This product can provide many benefits for babies, from protecting delicate skin from diaper rash to helping keep a newborn's navel clean and dry. Petroleum jelly also works great as an all-over moisturizer, alleviates the effects of winter cold on delicate infant skin, and protects against various irritants like air pollution. However, parents must avoid excessive use because petroleum jelly can suffocate baby pores if used in excess.

Another common use for petroleum jelly is you will need to use it for lubrication when you are using the rectal thermometer. With proper application, petroleum jelly can effectively provide calming relief to your little one!

Pedialyte

Pedialyte is an electrolyte solution often recommended by physicians for treating infant dehydration associated with vomiting and diarrhea. It is also an important source of nutrients for infants, as it contains essential minerals such as sodium and potassium to help maintain the body's fluid balance. Pedialyte also contains simple sugars that may provide energy during illness and replenish electrolytes at a safe rate. Lastly, its balanced composition helps ensure that the infant does not experience a rapid transition from intravenous fluid back to nursing or bottle feeding, thus helping protect the health of infants in cases of dehydration.

Disclaimer - You should only use it for newborns when recommended by your doctor who also provides a dosage.

Diaper Bag

Having a baby requires a lot of planning and preparation. One of the most important items you will need to prepare is a diaper bag, which is essential for caring for your newborn.

A diaper bag provides all the comforts, supplies, and necessities to ensure your little one has everything they need while you're away from home. Let's examine why having a diaper bag is so helpful when you have a newborn.

- Organization and Efficiency - Diaper bags can provide much-needed organization and efficiency in caring for your baby. They come with designated pockets and compartments that help keep all your items organized and easily accessible! You won't have to worry about frantically rummaging through your bag, looking for something; everything will be neatly stored where you can find it quickly and easily.

- Convenience - Diaper bags are also incredibly convenient because they eliminate the need to carry multiple bags or containers filled with items for your baby around. Instead, you can keep everything in one neat package that you can easily carry wherever you go. This means no dragging about separate diapers, bottles, and wipe bags! Instead, everything will be in one place, making life much easier when caring for your little one on the go.

- Adaptability - Finally, diaper bags are extremely adaptable. Whether you're heading out on an errand or going on vacation, these bags have features such as adjustable straps, stroller clips, changing pads, insulated bottle holders, and even waterproof exteriors, making them perfect for any situation! So no matter what kind of excursion awaits you and your family, diaper bags are an indispensable accessory that will ensure your child is always well cared for.

Here's what to think about when choosing a diaper bag

When looking for a diaper bag, you should consider a few things. First, consider what features you want in a bag; do you need many pockets, insulated compartments, a changing pad, and a waterproof lining?

Second, consider what size you need; you want enough room for all your baby essentials but not so much that the bag is too bulky and heavy.

Third, consider your budget; great bags are available at various price points, so it's important to find one that fits your budget. Lastly, consider your style; look for a bag that reflects your style and is comfortable for you. With these tips in mind, you should be able to find the perfect diaper bag for you and your child!

Baby Monitor

A good quality baby monitor can provide peace of mind and help ensure your child sleeps safely and soundly. Although in those newborn stages, your little one may be glued to your hip, there will be times when the monitor comes in handy.

The first benefit of using a baby monitor is that it allows you to keep an eye on your baby, even when you're not in the same room. Most monitors allow you to check in on your child from virtually anywhere. Some models even come with apps that allow you to watch and hear your child from any location, whether it's across the house or across the world! This means that if you need to step out of the room for other tasks, you can rest assured knowing that your precious bundle is being watched over.

Another great thing about baby monitors is that they are designed specifically for use with babies. Most models come equipped with temperature sensors, two-way audio, night vision capabilities, and specially designed lullabies and nature sounds that can help soothe your infant while they sleep.

Some models even include air quality sensors so parents can quickly identify any potential hazards in their home, such as dust particles or carbon monoxide levels. Today there are even models on the market, such as the Miku, that can monitor your child's breathing pattern and notify you if something is wrong.

Finally, many modern monitors feature wireless technology, which makes them incredibly easy to install and use. It only takes a few minutes to set up most models. Once installed, they are simple enough for even the most technophobic parents to operate without any problems! Additionally, since wireless monitors have no cords or wires, there is less risk of tripping over cables or getting tangled up in cords—which is always an added bonus when dealing with small children!

Baby Swing

A baby swing can be a lifesaver for parents while also benefiting the infant by aiding digestion, lowering irritation, and relaxing fussy babies. A baby swing helps soothe an infant by providing a consistent rhythm that simulates the natural rocking motion felt in the womb. Its relaxing rhythm aids in promoting better sleep. Thus parents find this helpful for getting their little ones to fall asleep easily.

Additionally, the gentle rocking motion also helps reduce stress and can even boost brain development. Since baby swings are designed for comfort and safety, moms and dads can trust that their little ones are being taken care of while they take a break from parenting duties. Thus it's no surprise that parents love using a baby swing because it's convenient and effective at providing babies with an enjoyable experience while helping with overall growth and development.

Although some people may claim a baby swing is not essential, I beg to differ. I think new exhausted parents can benefit from using a swing. I remember how much of a difference using the swing was for both my baby and me, and I would not want to be missing a swing if I had to care for another infant.

Pacifiers

Pacifiers are a must-have for newborns not only for the sake of convenience but also because they can provide real benefits. Studies have shown that pacifiers may help reduce infant crying and the risk of sudden infant death syndrome (SIDS). Of course, pacifiers should be used carefully and according to your pediatrician's instructions. As a parent, you should ensure the pacifier is clean and sterilized and replace it after three months or when it starts to wear out. Pacifiers can play an important role in ensuring your baby remains soothed, healthy and safe.

Teethers

Teethers are great for infants because they provide a safe and effective way for them to soothe their sore gums and emerging teeth. Teethers can also help stimulate a baby's senses, helping them to develop motor skills and hand-eye coordination. Teethers come in various shapes, sizes, and textures, giving babies plenty of options to explore. They are also usually made with soft materials that are easy to clean and safe for the baby to chew on. Teethers are essential in helping babies become independent and develop good oral hygiene habits.

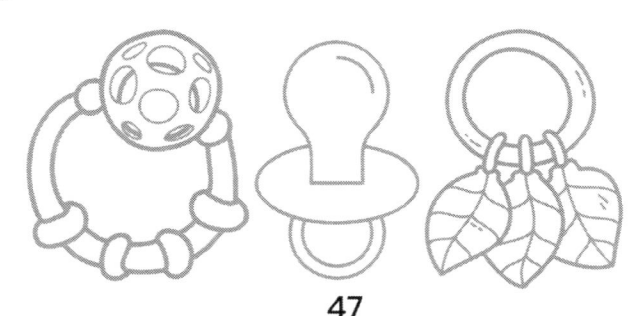

Nice to Haves

While a few essential items like diapers, clothing, and a car seat are necessary for taking care of a newborn, some additional baby products can make life with a new baby more comfortable and convenient. A nursing pillow can be very helpful for mothers during breastfeeding as it can provide added support and help prevent back pain. An activity mat can keep babies entertained and stimulated, promoting their development.

Baby rockers and bouncers provide a safe place for the baby to rest while parents need to take care of other tasks. Changing tables can also make diaper changes easier and more convenient, but it's important to note that a changing pad on a dresser or bed can serve the same purpose. Baby books can help stimulate a newborn's developing brain and foster a love of reading, while infant carriers and stroller accessories can make it easier to transport the baby.

Wipes warmers, bottle washers, and sterilizers are also nice-to-have items that can make certain tasks easier and more pleasant. However, it's important to remember that these products are not essential and can add up to be quite expensive. Ultimately, the decision to purchase non-essential baby items should be based on individual preferences and needs, and parents should always prioritize their budget and purchase items that are necessary for their baby's safety and well-being. Although these items are not something I would consider necessary, they are nice to have, and you should certainly consider adding them to your registry.

Nice to Have Items...

- Diaper Pail
- Wearable baby carrier
- Stroller accessories
- Wipes warmer
- Bottle sterilizer
- Baby toys
- Activity mat
- Jumpers
- Bath accessories
- Sound machine
- Rocking chair

Setup A Registry!

As a mom who has been through it all, let me tell you that one of the most exciting things about being pregnant is setting up your baby registry. It's a chance to dream about all the adorable outfits, snuggly blankets, and must-have gadgets that will help you care for your little one. You'll be amazed at the variety of baby gear available these days, and it's fun to explore all the options and choose what works best for your family.

Not only is setting up a baby registry a fun activity, but it's also a practical one. Babies need a lot of stuff, and purchasing everything on your own can be expensive. One added benefit of creating a registry is that your friends and family will want to help you by purchasing some of your newborn essentials. This can take some of the financial burdens off of you, which is especially helpful because childcare costs can add up quickly. In addition, you'll want to save all the money you can for when you have to start paying for childcare, so having loved ones chip in for items like diapers, wipes, and bottles can be a huge help. Overall, creating a baby registry is a fun and practical way to prepare for the arrival of a new baby. It can help with decision-making, gift-giving, and budgeting, making the transition to parenthood a little bit easier.

Chapter 3
Parenting as a Team

One of the hardest things to prepare for as new parents is getting on the same page with your partner. When couples are expecting a baby, it is important to discuss how you intend to approach parenting from the beginning. Having a shared parental vision and goals will give parents clarity and provide the necessary base to maintain harmony when dealing with parenting-related issues.

If this critical step is not made beforehand, arguments may occur amongst couples over who should take on specific tasks such as managing finances, setting boundaries, maintaining discipline, or taking care of the newborn. With so much love and emotion going around during those first few months, it's essential that couples discuss their expectations well in advance to create a secure and non-judgmental environment for both parent and child.

Practical Tips for Parenting as a Team

Communication

When a couple welcomes a new baby into the world, it brings about an entirely new set of challenges and experiences. Communication is the most important tool for navigating those changes and determining success as parents. Open dialogue from the beginning enables couples to work together in harmony, hold each other accountable to agreed-upon goals, and ensure that neither partner feels overwhelmed by the responsibility of parenting. By communicating openly, couples can better understand their individual and shared roles and take the stress off each other to be the right parent every time.

After having a new baby, you and your partner will be in uncharted territory. Stress levels will rise, and before you know it, you could both be at each other's throats if communication is not well established. It's important to pay attention to how you speak to each other, as your tone and body language can also influence the outcome of an argument.

==Set aside time each week to talk openly and honestly, without interruption or judging one another. Listen carefully to what each other has to say and be willing to compromise for the relationship to work best. When communicating, be mindful that there are two perspectives and try not to jump to conclusions before hearing the other person out. Respect each other's needs and desires, and come up with solutions together rather than focusing on who's right or wrong.==

We can create meaningful conversations that build connection and understanding within our relationships by utilizing these tips for effective communication.

Create Clear Responsibilities and Set Expectations

Setting expectations around sharing responsibility for a newborn can help new parents feel less stressed and more at ease in their caregiver roles. Sure, we can set expectations, but we can't always expect them to work out; not everything will go as planned. However, establishing expectations from the start allows both parents to have an equal say in decision-making while also relieving some of the burdens from one partner, if necessary.

Planning out who will take on what responsibilities limits misunderstandings and miscommunication and ensures that both parents are involved and knowledgeable about any decisions being made. It also informs both couples of their respective obligations, allowing them to set aside appropriate time to spend with the infant and each other as necessary.

Creating a plan ahead of time can help avoid stress and arguments down the line. One method is to assign specific tasks to each parent, such as changing diapers or handling dishes. This division ensures that responsibility is shared and prevents one parent from becoming overwhelmed. Additionally, tasks can be shared based on schedules or availability to ensure that both parents get adequate rest. For example, one parent could handle nighttime feedings while the other takes over in the morning. This rotation helps both parents get enough sleep, which is crucial when caring for a newborn.

Similarly, dividing other chores like walking the dog, bathing the baby, or doing laundry can alleviate stress and prevent arguments. This division of labor ensures that the household runs smoothly and everyone knows their role in caring for the newborn.

Having A Melt Down Plan

Get ready. As a new momma, you're going to face some tough moments. Not only will your little one have meltdowns, but you or your partner might as well. The transition from pregnancy to motherhood can be overwhelming. It's natural to have mixed emotions, and those hormones aren't making it any easier. Your typical parenting strategies may not work, and you may feel lost and unsure of what to do.

But don't worry, mama. I understand how you feel. You'll experience fear, panic, annoyance, frustration – the list goes on. It's a rollercoaster of emotions, and it's normal to feel overwhelmed. That's where your partner comes in. You'll need to rely on them for help and support. Don't forget to take a break and prioritize your mental health before you end up on the floor.

Trust me; you're not alone in this journey. Remember, with each tough moment comes a rewarding one, and the bond you share with your little one will make it all worth it. It's okay to struggle, but it's also okay to ask for help. So take a deep breath, mama. You got this!

Maternity Leave Doesn't Last Long... Plan Ahead

If you are a new mother in the US, then you already know that the United States is known for having some of the shortest maternity leave policies in the world. This can make it difficult for new moms to balance their work and family life. Therefore, as your maternity leave begins to wind down, it is essential to start planning for your return to work.

Many new moms struggle with the idea of returning to work and leaving their newborn in someone else's care. Being away from your child for long hours can be daunting, but it is important to remember that you are not alone. It is common for new moms to experience feelings of guilt and anxiety when they return to work. However, it is essential to remember that you are doing what is best for your family.

I have been fortunate enough to work from home and enjoyed having a nanny take care of my little one during the day so I could focus on work. Unfortunately, not all moms have the luxury of being close to their little ones while working full-time, so it is important to plan ahead.

It is crucial to start thinking ahead and building a plan with your partner. For example, will you put your child in daycare, rely on family, or will you become a stay-at-home mom? Each option has its own set of challenges and benefits, so it is important to weigh your options carefully.

If you decide to use daycare, you must start researching and touring facilities as soon as possible. Some daycares

daycares may have waitlists or limited availability, so it is vital to plan ahead. Additionally, it is crucial to consider the financial impact of daycare on your family's budget.

Here's a pro tip when it comes to choosing a daycare: Look for ones that offer cameras. It's nice to have peace of mind checking in on your little one to see them sweetly sleeping or getting cuddles. However, there are also daycare horror stories. Personally, I feel that when a daycare has careers, and the employees are aware of them, they will be more mindful of how they treat children.

If you decide to rely on family, it is important to have open and honest conversations about expectations and boundaries. It is important to ensure everyone is on the same page to avoid potential conflicts.

For additional food for thought, consider the financial impact on your family if you decide to become a stay-at-home mom. It may be necessary to make lifestyle changes or cut back on expenses to make this option work.

Overall, as a new mom, it is important to start thinking ahead and building a plan with your partner for your return to work. Remember that you are not alone, and many resources are available to support you. Finding a balance between work and family life is possible, but finding what works best for you and your family may take some time and effort.

How to Choose a Daycare?

If you are looking for a daycare, it's best to seek advice from people you know. Ask for recommendations from family, and colleagues, and check online reviews of daycare centers in your area. Ensure that the daycare you choose is licensed and has a good reputation.

You should also consider the location and hours of the daycare. Ideally, you want a daycare that is close to your home or work, making drop-off and pick-up times convenient for you. You should also check the operating hours to ensure they align with your work schedule.

Another thing that is important is to consider the staff-to-child ratio. Usually for infants, they tend to have one adult per four babies. This is important as newborns require more attention with frequent feedings and diaper changes.

When you've narrowed down a selection of possible daycare options, ask to tour them. Observe the environment and cleanliness of the facilities. If things are looking unorganized or dirty, that's probably a big red flag that children as also not being cared for very well. Ultimately, choose a daycare that you feel comfortable with, and that aligns with your values and priorities for your child's well-being.

It Takes a Village

You've likely heard the expression, "It takes a village to raise a child." Well, when you become a mom, you realize that whoever said that wasn't lying. During the newborn stage, becoming a mom can be overwhelming and lead to mental health issues. However, it is so important to recognize that having the support of family and friends nearby can help you adjust to your new life as a mom.

These people can offer emotional support, free up some time for self-care, and provide distraction during those long nights. Allowing other people to share in the joys and struggles of parenting also helps mom regain her sense of balance by creating an understanding community around her. There is no need to go through this difficult stage alone. Seeking help from family and friends provides peace of mind and can ultimately make the transition into motherhood more manageable.

It's also important to remember that asking for help isn't just about taking care of yourself; it's also about taking care of your baby. Studies have shown that infants who receive consistent, loving care from multiple caregiver's experience more secure attachment, which is important for their emotional and social development.

==Receiving care from various competent caregivers helps create a stimulating and nurturing environment for growing newborns.== A variety of voices reading aloud, singing songs, playing peek-a-boo, and speaking in different languages all contribute to a rich learning experience for babies. Having multiple people interact with infants helps little ones quickly build trust and comfort with many types of people, which is essential for the child's social, emotional, and intellectual development.

Early exposure to a diverse set of dynamics can help infants gain communication skills more rapidly, enabling them to make connections across cultures quicker as they get older. Considering the baby's individual needs while providing quality interactive experiences critical to their growth means that every new interaction brings new learning opportunities, whether between parent or caregiver. By building a supportive community around you and your baby, you are helping yourself and promoting your baby's healthy development.

Chapter 4
Packing for the Hospital / Birth Center

It's a good idea to start packing your bag for baby delivery around 35 weeks into your pregnancy. While it's easy to get carried away with packing every possible item, it's important to focus on the essentials.

A change of clothes for you and your partner is a must-have for the hospital stay. Opt for loose, comfortable clothing that is easy to move in and doesn't restrict your movements. You'll also want to bring a few snacks to keep your energy levels up, as labor and delivery can be an exhausting process. Don't forget to bring your insurance information, as well as any other necessary documentation, such as your ID and medical records.

It's also essential to bring a phone charger to stay connected with loved ones and make important calls. Additionally, make sure to bring copies of your birth plan to ensure your healthcare provider is aware of your preferences for labor and delivery.

While the hospital provides basic amenities such as pillows and blankets, bringing your pillow and a cozy blanket can add a touch of comfort and familiarity during your hospital stay. A book or magazine can help keep you entertained during the waiting periods.

Finally, it's essential to pack items for your baby's comfort and care. A going-home outfit, diapers, and wipes are a must-have. Depending on your preference, you may also want to bring a pacifier, a receiving blanket, or any other items that will help soothe your newborn.

Important Information

You've probably been doing a lot of research and putting together a birth plan. You want to remember this vital piece of information if you walk out the door without it. Of course, you already have an idea of how you would like the plans to go. However, having a written plan you can share with your partner, nurses, or doctor can help things stay on track when you may be in too much pain to think or communicate exactly what you want. Also, remember you may need to again bring your driver's license and your insurance information, so make sure you keep them in your wallet.

Snacks to Pack

First, you will be hungry, like super hungry, after delivery. So having snacks available for the few days you will be stuck in the hospital will be helpful for both you and your partner

Did you know you most likely won't be allowed to eat once you go into labor at the hospital? This is because if you actively push during the peak of your labor, you could end up feeling sick if the food does not stay down due to the natural contractions associated with giving birth.

So for a mother to safely give birth without experiencing any undue nausea or vomiting, it is recommended that no food be ingested during this crucial period. Furthermore, the hospital will want to ensure that all necessary medical interventions, such as medication, can be administered without any complications or hindrances.

Snack Ideas

- Trail mix
- Granola bars
- Your favorite chips
- Pretzels
- Bananas
- Peanut butter
- Dark chocolate
- Yogurt
- Pudding cups
- Muffins
- Beef jerky
- Dates
- Baby carrots
- Almonds
- Electrolyte drinks such as Gatorade or coconut water.

Keep in mind that you will need enough snacks for you and your partner. You don't want your partner to go out to grab something to eat when you suddenly need to push for the baby to come. Also, remember to pack things that don't require refrigeration. However, if you are a snack lover and want things that you require to be kept cool, you can always bring a small cooler with ice.

Toiletries

So I certainly don't expect you to try to look like an Instagram model right after delivery, but there are some basic hygiene items you will want to bring with you. Remember, after being stuck in the hospital bed and spending hours in labor, followed by intense pushing, you will feel as sweaty and gross as if you just ran a marathon.

If you end up getting a private hospital room, your room may include its own private shower, so make sure you can have a nice hot shower experience. Just keep in mind that you don't need to go overboard here because that will just mean more stuff to unpack once you get home, and you won't really have as much time for all that anymore.

Toiletries to Pack

- Hairbrush
- Toothbrush & toothpaste
- Deodorant
- Chapstick
- Hair ties

- Face wipes
- Shampoo
- Body wash
- Lotion

Entertainment

Going to the hospital for a delivery can be unpredictable; you may think you only need to stay for two nights but end up staying for five. So bring a few things to entertain yourself, such as books, magazines, earbuds, a tablet, a video game, or whatever else you fancy. Just keep in mind that you will mostly use these items until the baby arrives, but your partner will be getting the most out of entertainment items. Also, don't forget to bring any necessary chargers or anything else you need to keep the entertainment going.

Comfy Clothing

Keep in mind that even once the baby is out of your belly, your body will still be sore and swollen. Make sure you pack comfortable clothes that will be easier to get on and off before and after delivery. Additionally, you will want to bring nursing bras and granny panties.

I also recommend buying your own delivery gown because you may be living in that for a few days. The hospital will supply you with a delivery gown, but the fabrics are not the best. It's worth investing the extra money if you want to be comfortable while facing a nervous but exciting time during this hospital stay.

Comfy Clothing to Pack

- Comfortable robe
- Pajamas
- Slippers
- Cozy grip socks
- Going home outfit
- Granny panties
- Nursing Bras

Postpartum Products

The hospital will be helping you with the majority of your initial postpartum care, but you may also want to bring some of your own products. For example, adult diapers will be more comfortable than the mesh underwear supplied at the hospital. Another thing you may want to make sure you pack could be nipple cream if you plan on breastfeeding.

Postpartum Products to Pack...

- Peri Bottle - The hospital may supply you with one, but you can also purchase your own.
- Maxi Pads - You need the cotton pad, NOT the plastic ones, as they can cause irritation.
- Witch Hazel Pads - They help a lot with cooling, and you can also DIY your own.
- Perineal Spray - The hospital may supply you with one bottle, so buying extra is good.

- Miralax – You may want to bring this to the hospital because you will most likely be super constipated after delivery. I found Miralax to be the best product for me after I went through days of constipation problems.
- Nipple Cream – If you plan on breastfeeding, this can help soothe your nipples.

Packing Items for the Baby

The fun part of the packing will be packing up a few sweet items for the baby, like the first outfit he or she will wear. You will certainly want to make it memorable by bringing your swaddle blankets, pacifiers, baby bottles, and more. I know this is hard, but try not to go overboard. The hospital will also supply some of those things and the baby's first diapers.

Things to Pack for Baby...

- Going home outfit
- Onesies
- A small pack of diaper / wipes
- Receiving blanket
- Swaddles
- Baby bottle (optional)
- Car seat – have your car seat properly installed before going to the hospital.

See the FULL hospital bag packing checklist at the end of the book.

Leave a Review

If you are currently reading this book and found it helpful so far for preparing for a new baby, I would love to encourage you to leave a review on Amazon. Your review can help this content get found by other moms who need help planning their motherhood journey. Reviews not only give insight into the content of the book but also provide a sense of whether or not it's worth the investment.

I know that writing a review may seem like a small gesture, but it can have a big impact. By taking a few minutes to share your thoughts, you can help other moms find the support they need and show your appreciation for the author's hard work. So, if you have found this book helpful in preparing for a new baby, please consider leaving a review online. Your words may be just what another mom needs to hear to feel confident and empowered on their journey to motherhood.

Chapter 5
Pregnancy and Birth Complications

Any pregnancy is a special time for expecting parents, but it's also important to be aware of potential complications during childbirth. Knowing what to look out for and what can be done to minimize the risks can help ensure that mother and baby have a safe and healthy delivery.

Before birth, pregnant mothers and their healthcare providers must discuss potential risks associated with pregnancy, labor, and delivery. That way, if any problems arise during the birthing process, everyone will be prepared and know how to respond accordingly. Common complications during labor include prolonged labor, shoulder dystocia, infections in the uterus or pelvis, preterm labor, and preeclampsia (high blood pressure). It's also beneficial to understand what type of birth you plan on having, whether it's a vaginal delivery or cesarean section, to recognize any issues that might arise during the process.

Common Pregnancy Complications

The most common pregnancy complication is preterm labor, which is when labor begins before 37 weeks gestation. Preterm labor increases the risk of premature birth, which can lead to long-term health issues for the baby, such as breathing problems or learning disabilities.

Other common pregnancy and childbirth complications include:

- Preeclampsia (high blood pressure in pregnancy).
- Gestational diabetes.
- Placental abruption (when the placenta separates from the uterus prematurely).
- Infection.

Premature Birth

Premature birth can be incredibly risky for a newborn and their long-term health. Babies born preterm have an increased risk of various serious complications, from breathing problems to eye and ear infections. Additionally, studies have shown that the earlier a baby is born, the higher the risk of developing neurological delay or even brain damage. Premature birth can also cause extreme underdevelopment in vital organs such as the heart, lungs, and digestive system. While advancements in modern medicine have enabled doctors to treat many premature babies successfully, expecting parents should be aware of the potential risks involved in early delivery.

Preeclampsia

Preeclampsia is a dangerous medical condition often experienced during late pregnancy. It is caused by high blood pressure in the mother and can have serious risks for both her and her baby. Preeclampsia can be especially dangerous because it affects major organs in the body, including the heart, liver, brain, and kidneys. This can lead to complications such as blood clots, liver failure, and even stroke. Additionally, if left untreated, preeclampsia can cause a low amniotic fluid level, which can restrict the flow of nutrients to the baby, leading to fetal growth restriction and a risk of premature birth.

Without treatment or monitoring, preeclampsia can also cause seizures in the mother as well as premature birth or even stillbirth. Therefore, women need to recognize the symptoms of preeclampsia, which include headaches, nausea, vomiting, and swelling of the face and hands, and to seek medical attention if any of these signs occur throughout the pregnancy.

To prevent preeclampsia, women should attend regular prenatal check-ups, maintain a healthy diet and exercise routine, and monitor their blood pressure at home if advised by their healthcare provider. If diagnosed with preeclampsia, treatment may involve close monitoring, bed rest, medication, and in severe cases, delivery of the baby. Early detection and management of preeclampsia is essential for the health and well-being of both mother and baby.

Gestational Diabetes

Gestational diabetes is a condition that often affects pregnant women, caused by temporary changes in how insulin is used in the body. This can cause serious health complications for both the mother and her unborn baby, making it important to understand why it's dangerous. If not properly managed, it can raise the mother's risk of high blood pressure or preeclampsia during pregnancy. In addition, babies of mothers with gestational diabetes are usually larger, which may lead to difficulties during delivery or possibly require a C-section delivery.

Untreated, gestational diabetes can result in babies having low blood sugar levels after birth and being more susceptible to jaundice or breathing problems. Therefore, keeping a close watch on what you eat and other lifestyle habits during pregnancy is an important part of successful treatment. Medical professionals such as doctors and dietitians can guide expecting mothers to make sure they maintain proper nutrition while managing any elevated blood sugar levels they may experience during pregnancy.

Placenta Abruption

Placenta abruption is a severe complication that can occur during pregnancy, which involves the separation of the placenta from the inner wall of the uterus. The separation can happen either partially or entirely before childbirth, and it can cause significant harm to both the mother and the baby. Placental abruption is most common in the late second and third trimesters of pregnancy, but it can occur at any time during pregnancy.

One of the most significant risks associated with placental abruption is severe bleeding, which can lead to a lack of oxygen and nutrients in the fetus. This lack of oxygen can cause the baby to be born prematurely or even cause stillbirth. Additionally, if left untreated, placental abruption can cause maternal shock, which can be life-threatening for the mother.

It's essential for pregnant women to recognize the common signs of placental abruption, which include uterine tenderness and pain, abdominal pain or tenderness, abnormal vaginal bleeding, or backache. If any of these symptoms are present, it's crucial to seek medical attention immediately. Proper diagnosis and prompt medical treatment can help to manage the condition and reduce the risk of complications for both the mother and the baby.

The treatment for placental abruption depends on the severity of the condition and the stage of pregnancy. If the abruption is mild, bed rest and close monitoring may be all that's needed. However, if the abruption is severe or life-threatening, emergency medical intervention, such as a C-section, may be necessary.

Risk Factors for Birth Complications

Certain risk factors can increase your chances of having a difficult delivery. These include having had previous birth complications, being pregnant with multiples, being over 35 years old or under 17, having chronic health conditions like high blood pressure or diabetes, being obese or overweight prior to becoming pregnant, smoking during pregnancy, and using drugs during pregnancy. Additionally, pregnancy after age 35 increases your baby's risk of chromosomal abnormalities, such as Down syndrome or Edward syndrome.

It's important to know warning signs that may indicate an increased chance of severe birth complications. Contact your doctor immediately if you experience any of the following symptoms before 37 weeks of pregnancy: headaches or vision changes caused by preeclampsia; contractions every 10 minutes that do not stop; vaginal bleeding; abdominal pain; decreased fetal movement; swelling in your hands or face; or a fever of more than 100 degrees Fahrenheit.

Your healthcare provider should be your most trusted source of information regarding childbirth. They will be able to explain all the possible risks associated with giving birth and provide steps to reduce those risks. During pregnancy, it's essential to have regular prenatal care to ensure that both the mother and the baby are healthy. This involves monitoring the mother's health and identifying any potential issues early on so that preventative action can be taken if necessary. Your healthcare provider will monitor your health by conducting routine physical exams, performing ultrasounds, and checking your blood pressure, weight, and urine samples at each visit.

One important aspect of prenatal care is receiving education from your healthcare provider about warning signs of various medical conditions that could occur before or after delivery. Another medical condition that may occur after delivery is hemorrhage, which is excessive bleeding after childbirth. Your healthcare provider will provide education on the warning signs of hemorrhage, which include heavy bleeding, dizziness, and rapid heartbeat. They may also explain the steps that need to be taken if a hemorrhage occurs, such as immediate medical attention and intervention.

In order to prepare yourself for potential complications during childbirth, there are several steps you can take beyond regular prenatal care visits with your doctor or midwife. Staying active is one of the best ways to keep yourself healthy while pregnant. Regular exercise helps strengthen muscles used during childbirth while increasing overall body strength so you're better equipped for labor and delivery. Additionally, learning relaxation techniques like meditation or yoga can help manage pain during labor as well as reduce stress levels, which are important for both the mother's and baby's health.

Chapter 6
Basics of Postpartum Care

The weeks and months following a child's birth are filled with joy and newfound responsibilities. But while moms tend to be focused on caring for their babies, it is just as important that they take the necessary steps to care for themselves. This is where postpartum care comes in. Postpartum care is a vital part of the recovery process for new mothers, so let's take a look at what it entails.

How Long Should Postpartum Recovery Take?

After giving birth, your body needs time to recover from the intensive labor and delivery process. Many mothers discover that it takes a minimum of 6-8 weeks for their bodies to fully heal from the strain of childbirth. Generally speaking, this timeline is considered an average and can fluctuate depending on a variety of factors, such as your overall health during pregnancy and whether any medical interventions were necessary or not.

As with any medical recovery timeline, it is important to consult with your healthcare provider if you have any concerns about postpartum healing or are experiencing symptoms such as heavy bleeding, pain in the perineal region, chest pressure, or unusual emotional shifts. With professional guidance and support from loved ones, postpartum recovery is possible sooner than expected!

Physical Recovery

Physical recovery after birth can be unpredictable, but there are some general rules that all new moms should follow to ensure that their bodies heal properly. The first step is getting enough rest and drinking plenty of fluids throughout the day. Eating nutritious meals and snacks is also important for replenishing lost energy and rebuilding strength.

Exercise can help speed up the healing process, but it's best to start out slowly with light walking or stretching until you build up your stamina. Additionally, it's best to avoid lifting heavy objects or engaging in strenuous activities until your doctor or midwife has cleared you. Finally, make sure you visit your doctor for regular checkups during this period to monitor your progress and address any health concerns that may arise.

Eating Well After Delivery

What you eat during the postpartum period directly impacts your physical recovery and emotional well-being. Eating nutrient-dense foods such as leafy greens, lean proteins, complex carbohydrates, and healthy fats will give your body the necessary vitamins and minerals to repair itself quickly and efficiently. It's also important to stay hydrated by drinking plenty of water throughout the day— at least eight glasses per day should suffice! Staying hydrated helps ensure your digestive system is working properly and helps remove toxins from your body.

Eating nutritious foods also helps boost your energy levels, which can be low after giving birth, and provide the necessary vitamins and minerals for you and your baby. Another benefit of eating healthy is that it helps keep your immune system strong, which is essential for fighting illnesses and infections. Overall, eating a healthy diet can help to support your body's natural healing process, helping you to recover more quickly and feel more like yourself sooner.

Vaginal Delivery Postpartum Care

Keep in mind everyone's recovery time from a vaginal birth experience can vary widely, so don't compare yourself to someone you saw bounce back on Instagram. You could be pushing for several hours to deliver an 11-pound bundle of joy or have a speedy 30-minute birth. It's clear each person's postpartum recovery will be unique. Although the exact details depend on their individual experience with labor and delivery, one thing is certain: Recognizing that "the postpartum period can be pretty rough" helps us all prepare for what lies ahead!

Vaginal Tearing

After childbirth, it is normal to experience vaginal tears due to the tearing of the tissue from stretching during delivery. It's common for first-time moms to encounter second-degree tears; I was sad that it happened to me, but it is more common than you think.

Here are the different degrees of vaginal tearing:

1. First-degree tear: A first-degree tear is the least severe type of vaginal tearing. It involves only the vaginal lining or perineal skin and does not extend to the muscle.
2. Second-degree tear: A second-degree tear is a deeper tear that involves the vaginal lining and the perineal muscles.
3. Third-degree tear: A third-degree tear is a tear that extends to the anal sphincter muscle. This type of tear is more severe and requires medical attention.
4. Fourth-degree tear: A fourth-degree tear is the most severe type of vaginal tearing. It involves the anal sphincter muscle and the tissue that lines the rectum.

While allowing some time for self-care and recovery, keeping the area clean with lukewarm water and patting dry after showering will help reduce pain, itching, and swelling in the affected region. Applying a cold compress may also provide relief. If needed, an over-the-counter anesthetic ointment can be applied to help soothe itchiness and burning sensations. A doctor should be consulted if symptoms persist or any signs of infection develop, as additional treatment may be necessary.

Expect Vaginal Soreness

After giving birth, it is very common for women to experience vaginal soreness or tenderness. This is a normal labor symptom due to the stretching and trauma endured during delivery. The healing process can come with some degree of discomfort, so knowing how to alleviate soreness and what to expect can help make an already tough time in a woman's life a little bit easier.

Fortunately, there are several different ways that a woman can find relief from this soreness, such as taking warm baths, trying different positions when sitting or walking, and wearing comfortable clothing that doesn't rub against the area. During postpartum recovery, it's valuable for women to remember to listen to their bodies as they heal and take care of themselves by taking steps like these that enable them to enjoy their post-birth experience instead of suffering through it.

Things you can do to reduce pain
- Sit on a pillow or padded ring.
- Take an over-the-counter pain reliever.
- Use a numbing spray such as Dermoplast.
- Use a peri bottle to keep the area clean by spraying warm water.
- Take a shallow warm bath.
- Use a padsicle to literally cool your vaginal area.

What is a padsicle?

A padsicle is a cooling, gentle treatment for postpartum discomfort. It involves making an ice pack with a sanitary pad soaked in a witch hazel, aloe vera, and unscented essential oil solution. This can be placed directly on the skin, where it numbs the area with cold and helps reduce inflammation. Many women have discovered that their bleeding and soreness are greatly reduced with consistent use, and their healing process is significantly accelerated. Padsicles are perfectly safe to use after vaginal births or c-sections, as they provide the warmth and soothing needed while preventing the transfer of any bacteria from a foreign object into the healing areas of your body.

Vaginal Bleeding & Discharge

It's normal to experience vaginal bleeding and shedding of the uterine lining after childbirth, known as lochia. The amount of bleeding can vary from a light, menstrual-like flow for up to six weeks postpartum, though most people see a decrease in flow after two weeks.

During the first few days after delivery, you may encounter large clots or a gush of blood from time to time. It's important to keep track of how much is normal for you and contact your healthcare provider if there are any concerns about increased or sudden changes in bleeding or if the amount seems excessive. In general, rest, plenty of fluids, and avoiding strenuous physical activity may help reduce postpartum bleeding.

Discharge is your body's way of getting rid of the old and making room for something new. Color ranges from deep red to pastel green, with odors that should be mild—but if you detect a stench or start feeling feverish, don't hesitate to reach out to your doctor! These might be signs of an infection needing attention.

Constipation After Childbirth

Constipation is an often-unspoken problem for women post-childbirth. As the body's hormones adjust back to a pre-pregnancy balance, disruptions in digestive health can arise, including constipation. For mothers dealing with this uncomfortable symptom, various treatments are available, ranging from dietary changes to over-the-counter medications. Again I'm going to drop in my recommendation for Miralax here.

It's important to talk to your doctor about new solutions that might be right for you, as consuming too much caffeine or increasing water and fiber intake beyond recommended levels could cause further adverse effects. Working with your doctor may also help diagnose any underlying issues that could be causing constipation symptoms, and preventative measures can be taken to eliminate it altogether.

Hemorrhoids

Postpartum hemorrhoids are an uncomfortable but surprisingly common side effect of childbirth. They're caused by the strain of pushing during delivery, which can also cause swelling and increased pressure on blood vessels in the anal area. These swollen areas become inflamed and, in some cases, result in protrusion of tissue from the anus, making wiping after a bowel movement excruciatingly painful.

Although rarely serious, postpartum hemorrhoids should not be ignored and treated as soon as possible with lifestyle changes such as eating high-fiber foods to support softer stools, sitting in warm water baths, or speaking with your physician about more intensive treatment approaches.

Pelvic Floor Issues

Pregnancy and childbirth can often result in damage to the pelvic floor muscles and other tissues, leading to changes in a woman's bladder and bowel control, as well as pain during intercourse. To ensure these problems don't persist after giving birth, women must attend regular check-ups with their healthcare provider to ensure proper recovery.

Postnatal exercises may be recommended to strengthen the pelvic floor muscles by engaging the abdominals; this will help rebuild strength lost due to pregnancy and childbirth. Additionally, discussing any potential problems with a healthcare professional can allow them to recommend things such as drugs or lifestyle changes that might assist in diminishing symptoms or even restoring continence.

What is Pelvic Organ Prolapse?

Pelvic floor problems can be caused by pelvic organ prolapse (POP), which can lead to urinary or fecal incontinence. Pelvic organ prolapse is a medical condition that affects an individual's pelvic region. It occurs when the muscles and ligaments that support the pelvic organs weaken, resulting in organs such as the uterus, bladder, or rectum dropping from their normal positions. In severe cases, the affected organs may congregate around the vaginal opening and protrude out of it.

Although pelvic organ prolapse can be caused by aging or childbirth, its underlying cause is often unknown. Treatment options are available through physical therapy, lifestyle adjustments, medicine, and surgery; however, approaches differ depending on severity and personal preferences. Doing Kegel exercises correctly will help strengthen your pelvic floor muscles. To do this exercise, you squeeze the muscles you use to control the flow of urine and hold for up to 10 seconds, then release. Aim to do at least three sets of ten repetitions a day.

Urinary Incontinence

Pregnancy and childbirth are momentous events, but physical changes can have lasting impacts. Urinary incontinence can be one of these, with women suffering from pelvic floor issues after childbirth often left struggling to take control of their bladder. In some cases, this is caused by weakened muscles or damage to nerves in the area. However, it should still be taken seriously as providing effective treatments can significantly improve quality of life. Lifestyle changes such as including regular pelvic floor exercises in a physical activity program are essential for management. However, if symptoms persist, consulting a doctor can help to find tailored treatment options, such as medication and surgery, that may provide the necessary relief.

C-Section Recovery

In the United States, one in three babies is born via cesarean section. For women who have had a c-section, postpartum care can be slightly different than for those who have had a vaginal birth. Whether you're planning for your first c-section or you would like to know more about what the recovery process looks like, let's break it down.

Pain Management

C-sections are major abdominal surgeries, and understandably, patients may be concerned about the kind of postoperative pain they can expect. After undergoing a C-section, it is natural to experience sharp and constant abdominal pains that can last up to two weeks following the surgery. The pain levels can vary due to positioning during the operation. Other pains may be experienced, such as backaches, discomfort when standing or walking for extended periods, or numbness in the legs due to pressure placed on specific nerves. Understanding these symptoms can help you better prepare for managing your pain and make your recovery much more comfortable.

The first few days after a c-section will be the most painful, and many new moms need pain medication to cope with the discomfort. Talk to your doctor about what kind of pain medications you can take while breastfeeding. If you're not interested in taking prescription drugs, other options, such as over-the-counter medications and herbal remedies, may help alleviate some of the pain. Cold compresses and heat pads can also relieve soreness and aches in your abdominal area.

Healing Your Incision

Your healing process will depend on the type of incision used during your c-section, either horizontal (bikini cut) or vertical (up and down). Healing time is typically around six weeks depending on your individual circumstances; however, total recovery from a vertical incision can take up to four months.

Healing a c-section incision requires special attention and care. To ensure optimal health, it is important to follow your doctor's instructions and take the recommended steps at home. Taking measures such as wearing easily adjustable clothing and avoiding heavy lifting anything more than 15 lbs for at least six weeks can expedite healing and decrease discomfort. Washing with mild soap and warm water twice daily can also help prevent infection. In addition, applying ice packs may reduce swelling and soreness. At the same time, over-the-counter medications like ibuprofen or Tylenol can help manage any pain you experience. Keeping the incision site clean and dry will ensure proper healing and speed up your recovery.

After a c-section, it's essential to monitor for signs and symptoms of infection. While uncommon, a small percentage of C-section patients can develop an infection in the incision or abdomen area. If such an infection were to occur, one would likely experience redness, pain, and/or drainage at the site of the wound. A fever greater than 101°F may also be a sign of potential infection. It is essential to contact your healthcare provider if any of these signs are present so that they can diagnose and provide appropriate treatment quickly.

Breastfeeding After C-Section

Suppose you plan on breastfeeding after having a c-section. In that case, it is important to be aware that it may take more effort than usual due to the physical restrictions associated with recovery. It's important to understand that milk production may be delayed due to hormonal changes after surgery, but that is normal. With patience and consistency in nursing sessions, milk production should increase gradually within two weeks post-delivery. Some tips that might help with nursing include practicing skin-to-skin contact with the baby immediately following birth and avoiding pacifiers unless absolutely necessary, as they can interfere with successful latching on at feeding times.

Try different breastfeeding positions:
- The Football Hold - The football hold is one of the most popular positions for nursing mothers. By using this position, the mother cradles her baby in her arm like a football or an egg with the baby's body lying on its side. The baby's head rests in the crook of the mother's elbow and can easily reach her nipple. This position supports the mother and baby comfortably while allowing them to maintain eye contact throughout breastfeeding. Its easy accessibility also makes it possible for moms to switch breasts without having to reposition the baby, making it a great choice for longer breastfeeding sessions. The key to successful positioning is finding a comfortable height for both mom and baby, as incorrect positioning may result in challenges such as poor milk flow or general stress for

both participants. With just a little practice and guidance, moms can expect success practicing this special breastfeeding bond using the football hold.

- Side-lying Hold - Lie on your side and place your baby on his or her side, facing your breast. Support your baby with one hand. With the other hand, grasp your breast and place your nipple on your baby's lips. Once your baby latches on to breastfeed, use one arm to support your own head and the other to help support the baby.

Similar Symptoms to Vaginal Birth

In addition to all the other things we just covered, you will still have a long list of symptoms also relevant to vaginal birth.

- Vaginal discharge
- Contractions
- Tender breasts
- Hair loss/skin changes
- Mood swings
- Postpartum depression
- Weightloss

Chapter 7
Navigating Your Mental Health

Although becoming a new mom can be an exciting and life-changing experience, it also causes great mental stress. This can have damaging effects if not taken care of in time. Your own mental health should be given paramount importance as an expecting mother. You must take steps to practice mindfulness and prioritize self-care during this period to maintain physical and emotional well-being.

Seek support from your family and friends, or consider seeing a therapist if needed. It is essential to practice open communication with your partner and share issues that you may feel are too overwhelming to handle alone. Remember that being mindful of your mental health will ensure a smooth transition into parenthood for you, your partner, and your little bundle of joy!

Your Self-Care is Essential

As moms, we always put others' needs before our own. We tend to forget how important it is for us to take time out of our busy days and indulge in self-care activities. We can easily become so preoccupied with our day-to-day responsibilities that we forget to manage our health and well-being. It is not selfish to have someone else step in to help while you step outside the house for a few hours and invest some quality time in yourself. We can use this special time for things such as catching up on sleep, reading a book, or simply just taking a walk.

Self-care is essential for keeping your mental health in check, and it's important to take advantage of any downtime you may have during the day so that you can always be your best self for your family. This was a mistake that I had to learn from. I remember trying to do everything myself because I did not feel like a "good mom" until I was 100% there around the clock. I remember feeling like I barely had time to eat because I was so busy trying to be everything for my baby. I was turning down requests from others for help and, in return, just sabotaging my own mental health.

I want you to learn from my mistakes and take the time you need. Remember, this is a lifestyle change, and you don't want to get stuck in an unmanageable lifestyle that will create too much stress. If that is the case, then you could be on a slippery slope toward depression.

List of Self-Care Ideas

1.Take a nap when the baby sleeps:
Ok, we've probably all seen the TikTok videos about how moms hate hearing about this, but don't completely ignore the advice. There will be days when you get the baby to sleep in the pack-and-play, and you take a nap on the couch.

2. Take a relaxing bath or shower:
I'm not saying the newborn stage is easy because it absolutely is not. However, compared to the toddler stage, one advantage of it is that a newborn will nap more often, allowing you to still do some of the things you enjoy if you have the energy. For example, a nice warm bath can be a great way to relax. One of the reasons I preferred a bath over a shower during this stage is that you can still hear the baby cry. When you take a shower, it is much harder to hear, and then your mind will play games on you, such as thinking you hear crying and repeatedly turning off the water to try to listen or running out of the bathroom half-naked just to find that your baby is still asleep.

3.Go for a walk or get some fresh air:
Going for a walk or getting some fresh air is an excellent way to take a break from the daily grind and recharge your batteries. Whether you're a stay-at-home parent or work full-time, a quick stroll outdoors can help to improve your mood and provide a welcome break from your daily routine. If the weather is pleasant, getting some sunshine is a fantastic way to get some much-needed vitamin D, which is essential for strong bones and overall health.

Additionally, being in nature and surrounded by greenery has been shown to have a positive effect on mental health and well-being. Going for a walk with your little one can be an excellent bonding experience and a way to get some exercise together. You can explore your local area, point out interesting sights, and enjoy the fresh air and sunshine. If your little one is too young to walk, consider using a baby carrier or stroller to keep them comfortable and safe. If you prefer to go for a walk solo, this can also be a great way to clear your head and get some much-needed alone time. You can listen to music or a podcast, take in the scenery, and focus on your thoughts and feelings. Taking regular breaks like this can help to prevent burnout and improve your overall well-being.

4. Take a yoga or exercise class:
Participating in an exercise class can be very beneficial for new moms. The more you move, the more you release endorphins which can boost your mood and reduce stress. Plus, it can be a social activity that helps new moms connect with other parents who are going through similar experiences. Additionally, regular exercise can help new moms regain their strength and energy after pregnancy and childbirth, leading to improved physical and mental health.

5. Read a book or listen to music:
One great way to indulge in self-care while caring for your little one at home is to read a book or jam out to some music. If you are like me and love to learn and feel productive, reading a few pages of a book in your downtime can feel great. Perhaps you are someone who prefers to move more, turn on some music, and you can have a dance with your baby.

6. Write in a journal or practice meditation:

Journaling can be a great form of stress relief for new moms. It allows you to express your thoughts, jot down your ideas, and process your emotions, which can be super beneficial during your postpartum period. Another reason why journaling is great is that it can serve as a tool for self-reflection and personal growth, helping new moms gain perspective on their experiences.

7. Get a massage or spa treatment:

If you didn't get a prenatal massage, treat yourself to a massage during postpartum. It feels great to be pampered, and you deserve it. Sometimes getting out of the house and treating yourself will energize you and help you return positively to provide better care to your family.

8. Schedule a date night with your partner or a night out with friends:

Honestly, having a date night can do wonders for new parents. It's common for new parents to get stuck in a rut and no longer find time to connect with each other. If you can arrange for a babysitter or family member to step in so you can have a dinner date, it would work wonders. It's also great if you occasionally go out and connect with your friends for a few hours. If you and your partner plan for this, you both can enjoy some of the benefits of your old life while adjusting to your new one.

9. Take up a hobby or a creative outlet, such as painting, knitting, or writing:

Taking up a new hobby can be a great way for new moms on maternity leave to reduce stress and boost their mental health. Hobbies provide a sense of accomplishment and a break from the constant demands of caring for a newborn.

Whether painting, knitting, or learning a new language, a hobby can be a creative outlet providing a sense of purpose and fulfillment. Additionally, participating in a hobby can be a social activity that helps new moms connect with others with similar interests. Overall, taking up a new hobby is a great way for new moms to prioritize self-care and make the most of their time on maternity leave.

10. Get a makeover:

Getting a makeover can be a great way for a new mom to feel recharged and rejuvenated. After months of pregnancy and childbirth, it's common for new moms to feel tired and run down. A makeover can provide an opportunity to refresh and enhance one's appearance, which can boost confidence and self-esteem. Whether it's a new hairstyle, makeup, or wardrobe update, a makeover can help new moms feel like themselves again and remind them to prioritize self-care. It can also be a fun and enjoyable experience that provides a much-needed break from the demands of parenting.

11. Practice positive self-talk and affirmations:

Affirmations can be a beneficial tool for new moms to boost their self-esteem and overall well-being. Repeating positive statements, such as "I am a good mother" or "I am capable and strong," can help shift negative self-talk and cultivate a more positive mindset. This can be especially helpful during the postpartum period, when new moms may struggle with self-doubt and insecurity. Affirmations can also serve as a reminder to prioritize self-care and acknowledge the hard work and dedication required in parenting. By incorporating affirmations into their daily routine, new moms can improve their self-esteem and build a foundation for a positive mindset.

12. Set boundaries and say "no" when needed:
Setting boundaries and learning to say no can be essential for new moms to maintain their mental health and overall well-being. As a new parent, it can be easy to feel overwhelmed and overworked, especially with the constant demands of caring for a newborn.

Learning to set boundaries and say no to taking on more can help new moms prioritize self-care and prevent burnout. New moms can reduce feelings of stress and overwhelm and focus on what is most important for themselves and their families by setting realistic expectations and limits on their time and energy. It can also promote a sense of empowerment and control over their lives, which is crucial during the transition to motherhood.

An Introduction to Postpartum Depression

Being a parent is an incredible experience, but it can also be tough, especially if you're a first-time mom. It's normal to have worries and doubts. However, if you're feeling extremely sad, lonely, and crying a lot, you might have postpartum depression.

Postpartum depression is a type of depression that can happen after giving birth. It's not just something that happens to birth moms, but it can also happen to surrogates and adoptive parents. Having a baby can cause many changes in your body and life, leading to feelings of depression. But don't worry! You're not alone, and it's not your fault.

As new mothers, it is critical to understand the signs and symptoms of postpartum depression (PPD). Shockingly, over 14% of women experience PPD within three months of childbirth, and up to 20% of women can experience PPD or baby blues within six weeks. Knowing what is happening to your body and emotions will help you recognize when you should seek medical attention and begin treatment as soon as possible.

What is baby blues?

Baby blues is a mental health condition that some women experience after giving birth. It typically occurs in the first week postpartum and is characterized by mood swings, anxiety, sadness, fatigue, and restlessness. While it often resolves on its own within two weeks of childbirth, it can be serious and should not be ignored. It is believed that the sudden hormonal shift after giving birth may trigger baby blues for many women. Additionally, stress, lack of support, or lifestyle changes are often contributing factors to the onset of this condition. Paying attention to your mental health after childbirth is important for mother and child. Seek help from friends, family, and professionals if you believe that you or a loved one are suffering from baby blues.

Symptoms of Postpartum Depression

Symptoms of postpartum depression can include but are not limited to constant sadness, overwhelming fatigue, difficulty bonding with the baby, anxiety and irritability, difficulties concentrating and making decisions, changes in appetite, and drastic mood swings. Many new mothers who experience these symptoms will feel embarrassed or ashamed to seek help. However, it is important to remember that it is an affliction that affects many women, and most importantly, postpartum depression can be successfully managed with proper medical care. If you or someone you know are experiencing these symptoms, don't be afraid to reach out for help because there are treatment options that may relieve the symptoms of postpartum depression.

The good news is that various treatments are available tailored to each individual's needs. Awareness of the real facts associated with PPD may prevent its onset or enable program participants to seek timely treatment, saving both suffering and expense.

Chapter 8
0-1 Month Old Baby

CRYING — Newborns can cry up to: **3** Hours Per Day

SLEEPING — Newborns can sleep up to: **18** Hours Per Day

EATING — **8-12** Feedings Per Day

DIAPERING — **10-12** Diapers Per Day

Caring for a newborn baby can be an incredibly joyous and rewarding experience. Research has shown that being a parent of a new child can cause your body to release endorphins, resulting in high levels of feel-good hormones such as oxytocin skyrocketing. Moreover, something magical can be found in observing a tiny life grow over time. Despite the sleepless nights and messes to clean up, this often comes with much joy as they enter into different developmental milestones.

Caring for a newborn requires patience, compassion, and unconditional love, which will bring immense satisfaction and elation despite the struggles that come along with it. So let's set up some expectations for what to expect in the first 30 days of life.

Newborn Crying

When a newborn is born, it is equipped with only one form of communication—crying. It is the only way for the baby to express its needs, wants, and feelings. For parents, it can be challenging as they learn how to respond to the crying while also attempting to decipher what their baby needs. But how much crying should you expect in a newborn's first month?

Crying is an important part of babies' development. It helps them practice making sounds and strengthening their vocal cords and muscles. It also helps them develop emotional regulation skills that will later benefit them in life; being able to control emotions, self-soothe, and regulate stress levels are essential skills that start developing from birth.

In the first month after birth, babies can cry for up to three hours per day (spread out across multiple episodes). This number can vary depending on the individual baby—some may experience more or less crying than others—but generally speaking, 3 hours per day is an accurate estimate for most newborns.

Of course, as a new parent, it is worrisome when your baby is crying, especially when they don't settle quickly. Let's cover the basic reasons why your little bundle of joy could be screaming at the top of his or her lungs.

Hunger

It's no surprise that hunger is one of the main reasons why newborns cry. Newborn babies have small stomachs, so they need to feed more often than older children and adults. Feeding every two hours is expected during the first few weeks of life. However, if it has been less than two hours since your last feeding session and your baby is still crying, try feeding them again, as they may still be hungry. Some babies will require more frequent feedings, known as cluster feedings.

What are cluster feedings?

Cluster feedings are an important part of newborn care. It is when a baby nurses very frequently in a short period before taking a longer rest period. This type of feeding allows them to take in more of the fatty milk needed for a healthy diet.

Cluster feedings can help satisfy their hunger quickly and provide them with essential nutrients for growth and development. They are also great at regulating both baby's and mother's hormones while helping the mom establish a good milk supply. Learning to recognize when your baby is cluster feeding can be an invaluable tool for both parents and caregivers. Knowing these patterns can help them become more sensitive to the needs of their little ones throughout the day, at night, or at specific times of the week.

I remember how hard it was to take care of a baby and myself without much sleep during those days. By the time I would feed the baby, feed myself, and do some pumping, it would already be time to turn around and feed the baby again. This can be exhausting, and if you are breastfeeding or pumping, this amplifies your levels of exhaustion. It is easy to feel frustrated in these early stages, so try to arm yourself with as much help as possible!

Dirty Diaper

Another common reason newborns cry is discomfort from a dirty diaper. Change your baby's diaper as soon as possible if you suspect this may be the cause of their fussiness. Some babies are just more sensitive than others. Some are only bothered by a poo diaper, while others cannot stand being wet. A clean diaper will help keep them comfortable and happy for at least a couple of hours until their next change is due.

Over Stimulation

Sometimes, too much stimulation can overwhelm a newborn and trigger them to cry in response. If your baby has been exposed to too much noise or light, try calming them down by dimming lights and lowering noise levels around them while speaking in low tones instead of raising your voice unnecessarily loud or shouting at them, trying to get their attention. Swaddling them securely also helps reduce overstimulation, providing comfort and security for infants who feel overwhelmed by the activity around them.

Tired

Babies require more sleep than adults—up to 16-18 hours per day! So if your infant seems cranky, try putting them down for another nap, even if they just woke up from one not too long ago—their tiredness could be causing excess irritability or fussiness that leads to tears! Alternatively, rocking or cuddling them while making gentle shushing sounds could also help lull them back into dreamland quickly without further crying!

If it seems like all baby's needs are met, and he or she is still crying uncontrollably, then the baby may be in pain. This could be caused by teething, a tummy ache, or something else. If your baby seems to be crying for more than 3 hours, that could also reflect their personality as every baby is different, or your baby may have colic. It's always good to have your pediatrician on speed dial just for reassurance or to know when the crying has become abnormal, and you should take the baby to the doctor.

What is colic?

Colic is a mysterious phenomenon that affects infants, typically during the first three months of their lives. It is characterized by long periods of excessive, inconsolable crying that start suddenly and may last for hours. Although it can be a source of anxiety for parents, the good news is that colic usually resolves itself before a baby reaches four to six months of age. Unfortunately, colic has no known cause and no definitive cure, but there are still methods to soothe and comfort an affected baby through this difficult period in their life.

How do I know if my baby has colic?

Knowing if your baby has colic can be tricky, as the symptoms can sometimes mimic those of other illnesses or conditions. Generally speaking, babies with colic often display excessive and inconsolable crying that lasts longer than three hours at a time. They may also draw their legs up towards their chest or clench their fists when crying. If you suspect your infant has colic, contact your healthcare provider for an evaluation. They may recommend various strategies to help soothe your baby, such as keeping noise levels low and providing gentle rocking motions or vibrations to reduce fussiness.

Newborn Sleep

In the first thirty days of life, babies usually sleep anywhere from 16 to 18 hours per day. This includes nighttime sleep as well as naps throughout the day. Basically, newborns sleep about 75% of their life in the early days. You can even feed them while they are asleep. While this may initially sound like good news, it does not make anything easier on Mom. Sure, the baby will be sleeping a lot, but he or she will frequently wake to feed. Remember that they have small tummies and will require more frequent feedings. So, don't be surprised when the little one sleeps for an hour and then cries again due to hunger.

- Daytime sleep - Your baby can sleep anywhere from 15 minutes to 3 hours in one napping session. You can expect this to occur 3-5 times throughout the day.
- Nighttime sleep - Your baby can sleep about 2-4 hours per nighttime sleeping session.

- Wake Windows - Typically, in the first six weeks of life, normal wake windows can be 30 minutes to an hour and a half.

Every baby sleeps differently, just like adults. Some might doze off within 30 minutes of being awake, while others can stay alert for up to an hour! This colorful range of sleep patterns allows each little one to develop their own unique routine in the early months.

Feeding

Feeding your newborn can feel like a full-time job for any new parents out there. Newborn babies often eat 8-12 times in 24 hours - that's pretty frequent! Fortunately, their tiny stomachs can surprisingly hold quite a bit in those feedings. Of course, those little eating machines need all the nutrients those feedings provide to grow, so have no fear - it's totally normal to see your baby demanding meals every few hours!

In the newborn phase, babies rely on only breast milk or formula for nutrition. This can be direct from the mother or through a bottle. If you choose to breastfeed, the first milk that comes in is known as colostrum, packed with antibodies and other nutrients that help build a strong immune system. Your milk will start to come in a few days after birth, and you will be able to produce more of a liquid-based substance.

Babies should be fed around 8-12 times in 24 hours, and feedings should be around every two to three hours. For those of you moms who, like me, want to know if the baby is getting enough to drink, here is what you should aim for.

- First Week of Life - 0.5 - 1oz of milk per feeding
- 1-2 Weeks of Life - 1-3 oz of milk per feeding
- 2-4 Weeks of Life - 2-4oz of milk per feeding

> **NOTE**
>
> If you are breastfeeding directly, there is no way to measure how much the baby is eating. You can usually log how long the baby is attached to the nipple, and you should rotate so that both breasts are fed on at each feeding.

Should I set a feeding schedule?

No, this initial phase is too early to expect your baby to eat at certain times. Instead, simply follow the baby's hunger cues and offer the breast or a bottle when you think they need it.

What about spitting up?

It's actually normal for a baby to spit up small amounts of milk from time to time. This amount can range anywhere from an entire batch of milk that the baby has consumed to tiny droplets that don't require changing their clothes. That being said, excessive spitting up can be a sign of gastroesophageal reflux (GER), and parents should consult with their doctor if their baby is spitting up large amounts regularly.

Newborn Hunger Cues

Recognizing hunger signs in newborns is essential to being a new parent. Thankfully, research has shown that the way your baby behaves can indicate their need for food. Some of the typical signs include turning their head towards a feeding source, making sucking motions, and even licking their lips. However, it is important to know that each baby may express hunger slightly differently and steadily watch their behaviors while learning to understand them.

Some of the cues include the following:

- Rooting around your chest as if they are looking for the nipple.
- Putting their fist in their mouth.
- Opening and closing the mouth.
- Smacking or licking their lips.
- Fussing or crying.

As a new parent, it can be difficult to spot the signs early. If your baby starts to distress cry because they are hungry, it's even more difficult to calm them so that you can get them to feed. Keep doing your best to look for hunger cues, as early detection is the key to keeping mom and baby under less stress.

Diapering

Newborns tend to go through quite a bit of diaper change, sometimes an astonishing 10-12 per day! It can be easy to underestimate just how many diapers you will require with a newborn. Newborns typically outgrow the newborn diaper size after about one month, so it is crucial to keep that in mind when estimating how many you need for their first few weeks of life.

Diaper Sizes

- Preemie Diapers – These are diapers designed for babies weighing less than 6 lbs.
- Newborn Diapers – These are designed for babies weighing 10 pounds or less
- Size 1 Diapers – These are designed for babies weighing between 8 and 14 pounds.

Having some newborn sizes and size one diapers before your little one arrives is a good idea. Most babies born between 38 - 40 weeks generally weigh between 6 - 9lbs. So you can likely expect your baby to use newborn diapers in the first one or two months of life before you need to size up.

Baby Poop

Get ready to have to deal with a lot of dirty diapers. Sometimes you never know what to expect. However, that first baby poop is one, you will likely remember. This initial stool, commonly referred to as meconium, is often thick and sticky in texture with a dark green or black coloration. Though it may look disgusting, it is completely normal and nothing you have to sound the alarm about.

After the meconium has passed, any subsequent poops may still look questionable in color, but again this is normal. The color and texture of a newborn can vary depending on a few factors. One thing to keep in mind is that breastfed babies' poo can be quite different in texture and color from that of formula-fed babies.

How Often Should a Newborn Poop?
This can vary, but during the first week of life, you should notice an increase in dirty diapers daily. For example, your baby should poop once on day one of life. On day two of life, your baby should poop twice. On day three, the baby should go three times. This pattern of increased pooping usually slows down after the first week. On average, newborns will poop five times in 24 hours.

What if My Baby is Constipated?
Your baby is less likely to become constipated if he or she is breastfed, but it can happen. Formula-fed babies are more prone to constipation because the manufactured formula is not as easily digestible by a newborn. If your baby has not had a poop in over 48 hours, checking in with your pediatrician could be a good idea. If it has not gotten to that point yet, but you want to provide relief at home, you can try increasing liquids, giving gripe water, doing a light tummy massage, or cycling the baby's legs to help with natural movement and digestion.

Developmental Milestones
Monitoring developmental milestones in newborns is a critical factor in the early detection of individuals who may require additional support and care. These milestones provide insight into a child's overall intellectual, emotional,

Developmental milestone activities, such as learning language and demonstrating motor skills, help doctors determine whether the infant has any underlying health problems related to development. Keeping track of developmental advances is important to ensuring a baby's well-being and building the solid foundation that will carry them into successful childhood years.

WEEK 1

Within only one week of life outside the womb, your newborn has already established a deep bond with you. They have become instantly familiar with and comforted by your voice - which signals unconditional love to them! Even though they may not understand the words yet, talking is still immensely beneficial since it lays important groundwork for future language development in their brain.

WEEK 2

During the second week of life, your baby's vision starts to improve, and they are able to focus on objects 8 to 14 inches away. You may also notice your baby starting to track you as you move.

WEEK 3

Your baby is quickly becoming a snuggle buddy! They may not be the smoothest of dancers yet at three weeks old, but they are learning to appreciate and enjoy your embrace. They're comforted by being held in your arms and taking in all that familiar scent you give off – comforting for them and sure to fill any parent's heart with joy.

WEEK 4

Is your little one engaging in some vocal exploration other than just crying? Around the fourth week, many babies start to coo and make cute "ahh" noises when they catch a glimpse of mom or dad. Why not join the baby on their development journey by repeating back their sounds – it helps them learn!

Built-in Reflexes

Newborns have a productive day, even though they usually spend most of it sleeping! When awake, babies make reflexive movements from their developing nervous system. As this matures over time, these involuntary responses become conscious and purposeful.

- Root Reflex - The root reflex is an often-observed natural reflex in newborn babies. It typically is present at birth and involves the infant's tendency to turn his or her head towards any pressure applied to the cheek. This is an important developmental step because it encourages us to breastfeed, as the mother's nipple will be automatically pushed towards the baby's mouth whenever it searches for nourishment due to this reflex. The strength of this reflex can vary significantly amongst different babies but usually last about four months.

- **Sucking Reflex** - Once a baby is born, they begin to exhibit certain reflexes needed to survive. One of the most notable of these is the sucking reflex. This instinctive action helps newborns feed by stimulating their lips and causing them to open their mouths. When combined with a rooting reflex, where infants turn in response to gentle pressure on their cheeks, this can help them find nourishment from an available food source. The sucking reflex helps equip newborns with enough strength to successfully extract milk or other sources of nutrition from whoever or whatever firmly but gently touches their lips. While essentially all newborns demonstrate these automatic movements, both the rooting and sucking reflexes can differ in intensity from one baby to another.

- **Grasping Reflex** - The grasping reflex is a remarkable ability that newborn babies possess. It is an instinctive response to anything they can grab with their hands, involving the closing of their fingers when pressure is applied. Studies have shown that this prehensile capability has existed since prehistoric times and occurs in both humans and non-human species. Though a baby's muscle strength and coordination aren't fully developed yet, the grasping reflex allows them to cling to their parent or caregiver, which is a clear sign of attachment and bond building.

- **Moro Reflex** - The Moro reflex is an automatic response seen in newborns between the first and fourth months of life. It is believed to be an evolutionary development intended to protect infants from danger. For example, when a baby experiences a sudden loss of support or loud noise, they will extend their extremities away from the body before quickly bringing them back toward themselves with their palms facing up. This reflex usually fades by four months of age, but some babies may display it until they are as old as nine months. In addition, research shows that differing intensity levels may be correlated with issues such as attachment disorders, anxiety, low muscle tone, and other neurological development delays. Therefore, it is essential to discuss any concerns with your pediatrician.

Chapter 9
1-2 Month Old Baby

CRYING — Newborns can cry up to: **3 Hours Per Day**

SLEEPING — Newborns can sleep up to: **17 Hours Per Day**

EATING — **24-32 Ounces Per Day**

DIAPERING — **10 Diapers Per Day**

Congratulations! Your little one is officially one month old! How exciting! It has probably been a whirlwind of emotions, sleep deprivation, and tears. Still, the joy that comes with a new life is incomparable. A baby's first month of life is a fantastic experience as they learn so much every day. From learning to recognize different faces to providing gummy smiles and exploring their new world, it's truly a magical time. So, embrace the beauty of this moment and enjoy the sweet memories that come with it!

In this section, we will highlight some things you can expect as your newborn progresses to month two. We will cover fewer details in this round as you are probably gaining much information through trial and error and getting to know your little one better.

Crying

It is normal for your newborn to cry often after he turns one month old. Remember, typical newborn crying patterns usually amount to three hours daily. Typically newborns will cry because they are hungry or have dirty diapers. However, they will also cry when they are tired or overstimulated. Keep in mind if your baby is crying uncontrollably often and it's happening regularly, that is a sign of colic, and you should ask your doctor about it.

Here are some tips for soothing a crying newborn

1. **Swaddling** - Swaddling a baby helps them feel secure and warm, as well as helps to restrict their movements and prevent the startle reflex from waking them up. To swaddle your baby, lay out a large blanket, fold one corner over slightly, then place your baby face up on the blanket with his neck in line with the folded corner. Next, wrap one side of the blanket across your baby's body and tuck the edges under his back on both sides. Then take the bottom corner of the blanket, bring it up over your baby's body, and tuck it around his shoulder. Finally, wrap the last remaining corner of the blanket snugly around your baby's body. Ensure you do not wrap too tightly - you still want to leave enough room for air circulation!

2. Rocking - Many babies find rocking comforting because it simulates the motion they experienced during pregnancy. You can rock your baby by holding him securely in your arms or using a rocking chair or glider while seated on a cushion or pillow to keep yourself comfortable during long periods of rocking. You can also try using a swing or bouncer seat if you have one.

3. Pacifier - Pacifiers provide extra comfort for babies when they are feeling distressed and crying uncontrollably. They help satisfy babies' sucking needs while also providing extra comfort that may help soothe them when nothing else seems to work. Make sure you choose an appropriate infant pacifier size - look for "0-6 months" labeled pacifiers if possible!

Sleeping

Your little one will still need about 14-17 hours of sleep during the day after the one-month-old mark. Why do babies need so much sleep? Sleep is a necessary component of healthful development for newborns and infants. During sleep, the brain and body go through numerous processes to help promote physical and mental development. For example, during nighttime sleep, infants' bodies release hormones that are needed for growth as well as support of their immune systems. In addition, the development of skills such as language acquisition, memory formation, and problem-solving can be more easily accomplished when the infant's body is properly rested. Not that your baby will be speaking or walking any time soon, but sleep is helping that little baby's brain form connections to grow and improve.

Additionally, daytime naps help the hormonal balance that's essential for good mental health. Studies have also concluded that lack of sleep in newborns can lead to hormone imbalances, leading to physical complications such as hypertension in later years. Therefore, parents need to ensure their newborns get enough quality sleep that will enable them to grow up physically and mentally healthily.

Newborns are Restless Sleepers

You might have figured this out by now, but newborns are known to be restless sleepers, and their sleeping habits can be a cause of concern for new parents. It is important to realize that newborns' brains are not as developed as that of adults, so they do not experience full cycles of deep and REM sleep as adults do. This can lead to newborns waking up frequently during the night. Allowing for plenty of rest during the day is essential for helping newborns transition into good nighttime sleep patterns. However, it is important to note that babies will still wake up frequently throughout the night, even with these adjustments.

What Should I Do If My Newborn Isn't Sleeping Well?

Being a new parent can be tiresome, especially if your newborn is having difficulty sleeping. Although it may be more difficult for younger babies to sleep, there are several steps you can take to encourage healthy sleep habits. Establishing a predictable bedtime routine, such as an evening bath followed by reading or singing a lullaby, is important. Don't worry, we have yet to talk about sleep training, which will come a few months later, but it's important to try to adopt good habits early.

Parents should also consider creating a calming atmosphere to ensure the baby's environment is conducive to sleep. For example, drawing the blinds to block out sunlight and playing soft music softly in the background can help create a soothing and comforting space. Additionally, allowing your baby some time to vigorously move their limbs during playtime and walks throughout the day will help tire them out enough so that they are more inclined to snooze during the night. With patience and these beneficial tips in mind, you'll get closer and closer to both you and your little one sleeping through the night!

Feeding

Your little milk monster is still going to be on a feeding frenzy. Not much will change as the baby grows beyond the first month, except that he will likely consume more at each feeding. By the time your baby is eight weeks, you can expect him or her to be sucking down 24-32 ounces of breast milk or formula.

- 3-5 ounces per feeding is typical between 4-8 weeks

What should you do if you cannot produce enough breastmilk to meet the demand?

If you are not making sufficient breast milk, the best course of action is to speak to your doctor or a lactation consultant who can provide guidance tailored to your individual situation. They may be able to recommend strategies such as modifications to your breastfeeding techniques, supplementation with formula when needed, and rest and nutrition advice that can help increase the amount of breast milk you are producing. Additionally, contacting a local breastfeeding support group that can provide emotional support during this time may be valuable. Ultimately, talking to professionals who understand the breastfeeding process is the best way to ensure you have the information and resources needed to meet your own breastfeeding goals.

How to know if your little one is getting enough?

Feeding your newborn can seem like an endless task, but you can use some simple strategies to ensure they're getting the proper nourishment. Here are a few ways to tell if your newborn is eating enough and how best to provide good nutrition for them:

Growth Signs: Babies grow quickly, so it's important that parents can recognize signs of proper nutrition in their newborns. If your baby is gaining weight, has plenty of wet diapers, and seems alert and active during waking hours, then chances are they are getting enough food. If you ever have any concerns about your baby's growth or development (or lack thereof), it's always best to talk with your pediatrician or family doctor, who will be able to offer personalized advice based on their age and individual needs.

Falls Asleep After Feeding - Falling asleep after feeding is a common behavior among newborns. The act of nursing is not only essential for providing the necessary nutrition for growth and development, but it is also a comforting experience that can help soothe a fussy baby. Once a newborn is full and satisfied, it's normal for them to feel relaxed and content, making it easier for them to drift off to sleep.

Baby is Content - After a feeding session, it's essential to monitor your baby's behavior to determine if they are satisfied and have had enough to eat. One indication that your baby is satisfied and full is if they seem content and relaxed. If your baby appears happy and comfortable, it's a good sign that they have had enough to eat.

Overall you are doing great with your feeding routine. Keep in mind every baby is different, and it's important to learn your baby's individual cues and signals to determine when they are hungry or full. Regular feeding and weight checks can help to ensure that your baby is getting enough food and is growing and developing appropriately. However, if anything seems alarming to you, don't hesitate to contact your pediatrician.

Diapering

Are you already wondering when you can slow down on changing diapers? Well, I'm sorry to tell you that won't happen just yet. You will still expect about ten diapers a day after the one-month mark. Although it may seem like a lot now, once the baby gets older and more mobile, then it becomes a bigger challenge. So, for now, just embrace those frequent diaper changes before the little one can roll over or run away.

Are you wondering what size diaper you should use for your child? Well, many babies will be in size 1 diapers by the 8-week mark, but this also depends on the baby's size. If he or she was born a smaller size or born early, newborn diapers could still work.

Here's a quick recap on diaper sizing:

- Newborn Diapers - These are designed for babies weighing 10 pounds or less
- Size 1 Diapers - These are designed for babies weighing between 8 and 14 pounds.
- Size 2 Diapers - These are designed for babies weighing between 12 and 18 pounds.

While the diaper size recommendation based on your child's weight is helpful, it does not necessarily tell the whole story. So, how to know if your baby is in the right size of diapers? When the diaper looks snug in the waistband and leg cuffs for extended periods, it is time to go up a size. In addition, if there is frequent leakage that goes around these areas or if you notice gaps between your baby's skin and the diaper, then it's likely that it's time for an upgrade. It is also good to be prepared with a few extra packs of larger ones, especially at night, as leakages tend to become more prominent while they sleep.

Developmental Milestones

Between the first and second months of life, your newborn will begin to reach several important milestones. This includes developing the ability to recognize and respond to sound, including recognizing familiar voices and responding with facial expressions. Your baby's senses – touch, sight, hearing, and taste – will also sharpen during this time. For example, you may see your baby's vision focusing on objects or following movements. Additionally, head control generally kicks in during this time as well.

WEEK 5

As your little one matures, watch how their movements become increasingly coordinated and graceful. Encourage them as they discover new ways of getting around – why not try a gentle backward pull-up or see what happens when you let them gently hover above the ground with their tummy on your forearm? Remember that those neck muscles aren't quite there yet, so provide head support during any activity!

WEEK 6

As babies approach two months of age, they begin emitting their first heartwarming grin! They'll bring joy to your day by widening and brightening their eyes as the corners of their mouth turn upward.

WEEK 7

Your little one is starting to explore their senses and recognize cause-and-effect relationships; when they see a rattle, they understand that the jingly sound comes from shaking it. They're also beginning to appreciate colors more! Show them some bright shades with 3D objects for enhanced exploration and learning.

WEEK 8

As your little one grows, so do their neck muscles to help support their head! With practice and supervision, they can now lift up to 45 degrees. Encourage them even more by putting them on their stomach for some playtime each day – it'll help strengthen those important baby muscles!

Activities

Doing activities with a newborn helps establish important foundations for the future. Activities such as reading, singing, and talking boost the development of language, cognitive skills, and a healthy parent-child relationship. They also provide opportunities to identify developmental delays and health concerns as early as possible.

First, I highly recommend you continue the same activities we covered last month. Just to recap, that would be tummy time, baby massages, skin-to-skin contact, and singing to your baby. But now that the baby is growing, and we might want to mix things up a bit, let's uncover some more age-appropriate activities you can do with your baby.

Play Music

The impact of music on a newborn baby is significant and far-reaching. Studies have shown that early exposure to sound, especially music, helps infants develop sensory perception, language processing, and memory formation. Playing music to a newborn can introduce them to new sounds and enhance their ability to differentiate different types of sounds. As babies get older, they begin to recognize melodies they've heard before and even show responses to genres or instruments they enjoy or dislike. Introducing your baby to various types of art will inspire imaginative brain connections while encouraging learning in the process!

Dancing with Baby

Recent studies have shown that dancing with a newborn can shape a baby's physical, social, and emotional development in numerous ways. Infants can respond to auditory stimulation from an early age, which is why songs and nursery rhymes are so important for their growth. When dancing with a newborn, parents can provide this auditory stimulation through music and rhythm, which fosters motor skills development. It can also promote social interaction by encouraging bonding with caregivers through sustained eye contact and vocal communication like smiling or cooing. Lastly, it allows babies to be tactile by making contact with different textures on clothing by swaddling them up close or being held in various positions while dancing. Therefore, it is clear that engaging in activities such as dancing with a newborn comes with many benefits.

Mirror Play

One of the most important ways for a newborn baby to learn about the world is through interacting with those around them, including objects in their environment. Showing a newborn infant a mirror can help contribute to their development. It encourages babies to recognize themselves and their faces. Doing so helps their visual recognition skills, fine motor skills, and speech-language development as they develop self-awareness and are able to verbalize who they see in the mirror. Showing a newborn a mirror is an effective way to foster growth in vital cognitive milestones.

Chapter 10
2-3 Month Old Baby

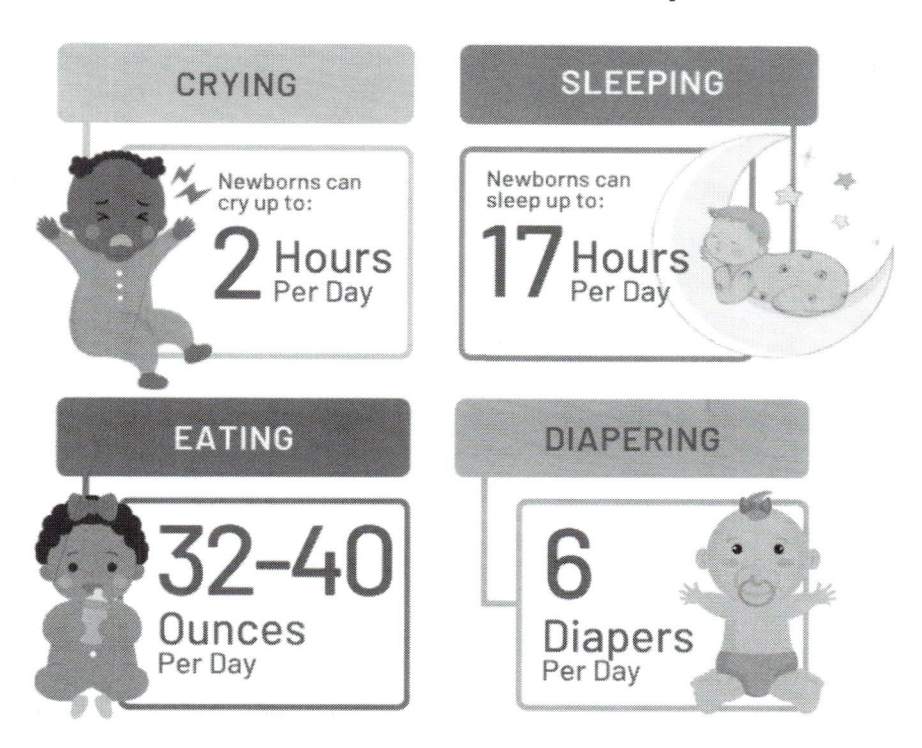

CRYING — Newborns can cry up to: **2 Hours Per Day**

SLEEPING — Newborns can sleep up to: **17 Hours Per Day**

EATING — **32-40 Ounces Per Day**

DIAPERING — **6 Diapers Per Day**

How are you doing, mama? By this stage, you must be exhausted and over-changing so many diapers around the clock. I'm sure you are wondering when this newborn stage will end. Well, I have some good news for you. The newborn stage of a baby's life usually ends at around the 3-month mark. At this time, babies are beginning to gain control of their head movements, interact and respond more actively with parents and caregivers, and smile in response to stimuli. ==During this development period, a baby will also demonstrate increased coordination by reaching out and grasping at objects.==

After three months, the infant has begun to transition from an immobile and predominantly passive state into a more independent one. This important milestone informs caregivers that it is time to start introducing activity-based learning experiences that cater to the developing parts of their brain to further growth and emotional well-being throughout childhood. So, let's buckle up for one more month of what feels like endless work in this newborn stage.

Crying

It's normal for newborns to cry, but parents should be aware that this crying should diminish significantly by three months old. Crying can indicate various issues, such as hunger, discomfort, or illness, so parents need to assess their children and respond accordingly when they hear them in distress.

As you become more familiar with your baby's cues, you will learn how to help reduce crying. Additionally, ensuring that your newborn's needs are met regularly can help prevent prolonged bouts of crying. You can still expect the baby to wake up from a nap and cry, but by now, you likely know how to soothe the crying much more quickly than before. However, if the crying does not decrease at three months old, it could be a sign that something else is wrong, and parents should consult their pediatrician.

Crying vs. Fussing

Understanding the difference between newborn crying and fussing can be an important bit of knowledge for new parents. Crying is a baby's primary communication method, so it should not be ignored. Fussing, on the other hand, is often a sign of hunger or fatigue.

Unfortunately, distinguishing between the two can be more challenging because newborns often cycle back and forth between bouts of fussiness and crying. A good tip to help differentiate is that if crying becomes louder and more consistent over time, your baby may need something from you, such as food, a diaper change, or comfort. Understanding the nuances of newborns' cries versus fussing can provide better insight into how to respond effectively to your little one's needs.

Sleeping

The sleep routine likely won't change significantly. We still expect a 2-month-old baby to aim for about 14-17 hours of sleep daily. However, as your little one grows, you can also expect your wake windows to last longer. For example, if last month your little one was sleeping 17 hours a day and is now down to only 14 hours per day, that is also okay.

Although you may be desperate to return to a normal adult sleeping schedule, you should not plan to sleep-train your baby yet. Sleep training is usually reserved for children between 4-6 months, and believe me, that is not easy!

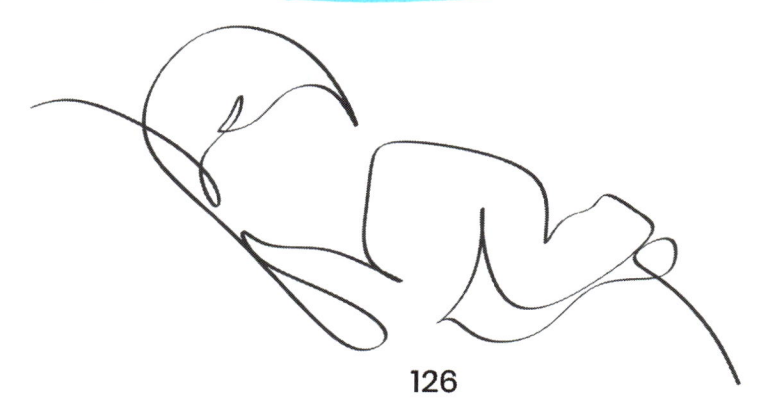

Here are some tips to help your 2-month-old sleep better at night.

Start a Bedtime Routine

A good bedtime routine is essential in helping your baby (and you!) sleep better. Start by establishing a regular bedtime—say 8 pm—and stick to it every night. Then, an hour before this time, begin winding down activities and start preparing your baby for bedtime with calming activities like bath time or reading stories together. A warm bath helps relax muscles while reading stories or singing lullabies have been proven to calm young babies and help them drift off into dreamland faster. You may also consider using white noise or soothing music in their room as background noise as they fall asleep.

Create Sleep Cues

Another way to help your two-month-old learn how to sleep better at night is by creating sleep cues. These signals will tell your baby it's time for them to go to sleep, such as changing into their pajamas or dimming the lights in their bedroom. These cues will help them differentiate between daytime fun and nighttime rest. Additionally, try not to pick up your baby immediately when they cry out during the night; instead, wait a few minutes first before responding, if possible, so that they understand that nighttime is meant for sleeping and not playing around!

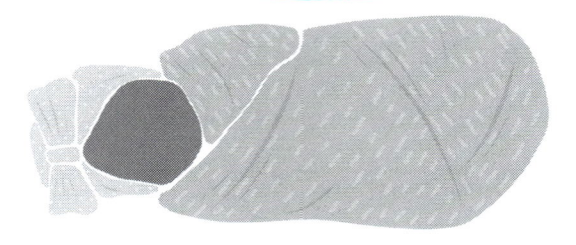

Follow Their Lead

At this age, babies learn best when their parents or caregivers give them lots of individual attention and patience. When attempting to establish good sleeping habits with your two-month-old, follow their lead as much as possible and listen to what works best for them in terms of sleep environment or routine changes that may need to be adjusted over time. This could mean adjusting their bedtime slightly earlier or later than usual, depending on how well they sleep each night; just remember that consistency is key here!

Feeding

- Two-month-olds should eat significantly more than they did in the first few weeks of life.
- Formula-fed babies usually require 4-5 ounces per feeding every 3-4 hours.
- Breastfed babies consume fewer ounces but still need to eat at least eight times a day.

It is important to pay attention to baby cues, as some infants may need more or less depending on their needs. If your baby appears to be hungry sooner than expected, consider offering them a small snack like an extra ounce of formula or a few additional minutes of breastfeeding between regular feedings.

Worried Your Newborn is Consuming Too Much?

Overfeeding your infant can lead to serious health concerns, including childhood obesity and an increased risk of certain diseases later in life. To ensure you're giving your baby enough food without overfeeding, look for signs that they are full.

Common signs include turning their head away from the bottle or breast while feeding, making slow or irregular sucking motions, or having several long pauses during feeding. Breastfed babies often eat less frequently than bottle-fed babies due to natural indications such as hunger hormones and satiety signals. Listen to your baby's appetite: when they reach their fill, stop feeding them and try again in another couple of hours if necessary.

Worried That Your Newborn Is Not Eating Enough?

I remember being worried my little one was not drinking enough formula. He was initially on track per the feeding schedule, then slowed down and became more of a "snacker." This can be alarming for any parents, but it does happen. Your baby might go from drinking 5oz in one feeding down to suddenly consuming only 2.5 ounces. I can't promise it won't drive you crazy, but it is okay as long as they are gaining weight and following their growth curve.

You are still a new mom, and you have plenty to worry about. As long as you offer your little one food, follow their cues. Sometimes newborns and infants go through phases where some days they want more and others they want less. If you are bordered, connect with your pediatrician to ensure your baby is developing well.

Diapering

The number of diapers you will go through in a 24-hour window should start to reduce. An estimated two-month-old baby will use around six diapers per day. However, this number may vary depending on how frequently they eat and their individual physiology. By this time, most babies will be in size 1 or 2 diapers, so make sure you stock up on the next size if they are getting close to moving into a different size range.

- Newborn Diapers – These are designed for babies weighing 10 pounds or less
- Size 1 Diapers – These are designed for babies weighing between 8 and 14 pounds.
- Size 2 Diapers – These are designed for babies weighing between 12 and 18 pounds.

Should I Switch Diaper Brands?

Diaper brands can make a big difference in how healthy and comfortable your little one is, so it's worth considering a switch if you think the current brand isn't meeting your needs. Start by talking to other parents you trust who have made the switch, or read reviews of different diaper brands online to get an idea of how other parents feel about them. Consider the diaper's absorbency, comfortability, or environmental friendliness; not all diapers are created equal!

I started with Costco's Kirkland diapers as they were very similar to Huggies and fit my smaller-sized baby better. However, I eventually switched to Pampers because Pampers did not have an elastic-style waist which seemed more challenging to get on. One of the other things I liked about Pampers is that they do not smell as bad. Other diapers I tried tended to retain a strong urine odor, especially overnight.

Developmental Milestones

Two-month-old infants typically have somewhat predictable milestones they strive to meet during this stage. Physically, these include tracking objects with their eyes and moving their arms and legs in all directions. In addition, they may coo and gurgle and possibly even laugh at this age!

Cognitively, babies may recognize familiar faces, respond positively to different pleasant sensations, and become more vocal about their needs. Parents must nurture these changes by talking to babies as much as possible, giving them appropriate visuals for stimulation, playing simple games such as peek-a-boo, and actively engaging with them as much as possible. Understanding developmental milestones is essential for forming healthy lifetime habits; this stage just being the first!

WEEK 9

Your baby is already learning to communicate! Sounds are particularly interesting, with high tones and pitches taking center stage. They also love watching you speak - gazing intently at your mouth as if deciphering every syllable. Who knows? They may even be cooing back in response!

WEEK 10

As your baby approaches their 10th week, he or she might just surprise you with the ability to pick out familiar faces amongst a group of people. If someone close comes near them, expect wide eyes and enthusiastic movement—a sure sign that your little one is honing those social skills! It's time to get family-friendly activities going. Why not bring them along for dinner or take advantage of carrier slings while around the house? With this new skill under their belt, accomplishing daily duties will be like having another member in tow.

WEEK 11

As your little one continues to grow and explore, they're now more awake than ever! They may appear captivated while learning about the world around them. However, if their eyes begin to wander or they look away altogether – it could mean that either there's too much going on for comfort or simply that something else has caught their attention & curiosity - so don't worry if this happens; switch up activities accordingly and see what captures those sparkly peepers of theirs!

WEEK 12

During this exciting development phase, your baby is discovering a delightful new world! They've likely just realized they have hands and are keen to explore their capabilities. Encourage further examination by giving them stimulating experiences in the form of tactile objects like crinkle books or rubber toys – watch as their curiosity takes over!

Activities

Spending quality time doing activities with your baby is one of the greatest gifts you can give them. It is an excellent form of bonding and a great way to nurture your relationship and creates wonderful learning opportunities. There are endless ways to stimulate their minds through active play, from exploring their environment and engaging their senses to strengthening sensory-motor skills and boosting social development by providing them with different objects to grasp and manipulate. Doing activities together also provides meaningful conversations for both parent and child alike, creating lasting memories that can be cherished for a lifetime.

Continue with all of the other activities we outlined previously. They all play a key role in helping your little one develop. Skin-to-skin, tummy time, singing, baby massage, playing music, dancing with the baby, and showing the baby a mirror were among the activities. Now we will add new activities that your child is ready for to the ones already in place.

Object Tracking

Object tracking is a crucial milestone to watch for in infants. It plays an important role in their cognitive development and has been shown to be linked to the successful processing of information later on in life. Object tracking begins as early as one month after birth, and by four months, babies should have developed the ability to follow objects with their eyes.

Tracking an object demonstrates that an infant has the motor skills necessary to turn his or her head, most essential that the neck muscles are strong enough. Additionally, it shows that the baby can process input from nearsightedness and farsightedness, which can affect visual performance throughout his or her life. As a result of its importance, parents and caregivers need to pay attention to object tracking as part of a newborn's growth and development.

To perform this activity, simply grab a small to a medium-sized object like a block, book, or stuffed animal and slowly move it in front of your baby from left to right. Notice their eyes tracking the object. If you are seeing this, it's an excellent sign they are on track with this developmental milestone.

Activity Gym Time

Place your baby down on an activity mat or an activity gym for a few minutes. Activity mats are an effective way to foster physical, mental, and social development in two-month-old babies. Activity mats or gyms contain several different tactile elements like textures, shapes, and colors, encouraging the discovery of new things by stimulating the baby's senses. Moreover, some mats come with removable toys or lights, which make exercising even more enjoyable and can stimulate babies as they move around. Activity mats also encourage gross motor skill development, such as grasping and shaking, which help strengthen muscles needed to crawl later on in development. They also provide opportunities for social interaction when parents or caretakers join the fun too!

Funny Faces

Making funny faces like sticking your tongue out or scrunching up your nose is a great way to entertain your little one, but it also has other learning advantages. Facial expressions like smiling, sticking out one's tongue, and wrinkling up your nose help engage babies socially and strengthen their neural connections. This has a domino effect, allowing babies to better recognize emotions, acquire language, build memory recall capabilities, develop problem-solving skills, and interact with their caregivers more naturally. Making funny faces is an easy way for caretakers to help foster a baby's growth!

Reading Books

Reading books to a newborn is an excellent way to foster an early love of learning and literacy. Sharing stories with a baby enriches their language development by introducing new words and increasing communication between parent and child. Reading can help toddlers explore emotions, such as laughing over silly stories or empathizing with a sad character. Reading benefits a child's cognitive development because it allows them to train and increase memory recall by creating connections between the pictures in the book and real-life experiences.

Conclusion
Mama, You've Got This!

Mama, you've got this! Being a parent is undoubtedly one of the most challenging and fulfilling experiences of your life. But it's also perfectly normal to feel overwhelmed, anxious, and unsure of yourself in the beginning. Every mother has the strength and resilience to overcome the obstacles that come with raising a child. Whether it's sleepless nights, endless diaper changes, feeding challenges, or tantrums, you are doing a great job, and your efforts are appreciated.

That's why I want to encourage you and remind you that you are not alone, and you've got this! I celebrate your strength and dedication as a mother and encourage you to keep going, even when the going gets tough. Let's quickly recap what we've learned so far and highlight some important tips to guide you on this journey.

As you've already learned from reading this book, there are many things to prepare for before you even bring your baby home. I just wanted to remind you not to overlook the importance of baby-proofing your home, and this should be done around the same time you are getting the nursery ready. Thinking about safety in advance will help you be more mindful and well-prepared for the unknowns you will definitely experience ahead. It's important to note that baby proofing is an ongoing process, as your baby will grow and become more mobile, so you'll need to continually reassess and make adjustments.

By baby-proofing your home early on, you'll have peace of mind knowing that you've taken steps to ensure your baby's safety. Knowing what exactly to buy for your little one is another common challenge moms face, but don't worry, I've got you covered. If you have the paperback or ebook version of this book, then you can simply jump to the end of it and find the entire checklist. Feel free to print it off or simply check the boxes directly in the book as you acquire your baby essentials. I've also included a full checklist of things you should pack for your hospital or birthing center stay to also keep it easy and organized for you, mama!

Now that you have an idea of all the things required to bring a baby home, don't delay starting your registry. The truth is babies are expensive, and the more help you can have friends and family pitch in to cover associated costs, the better. From buying baby gear and furniture to stocking up on diapers, formula, and other essentials, the costs can quickly add up. That's why it's important to start your registry early so that you can begin gathering the things you'll need for your new arrival. By creating a registry, you can let your loved ones know what items you need and which ones you would like to receive as gifts.

Starting your registry early also gives you plenty of time to research the products you want and compare prices. You can read reviews, ask for recommendations from other parents, and even test out products in stores to make sure you're making the best choices for your baby.

One of the most important takeaways from this book on newborn care is the crucial role that teamwork plays in providing the best care for your baby. Parenting is an immense responsibility, and it can be incredibly challenging to navigate alone. That's why it's essential to work as a team with your partner or support system to provide the best care for your newborn.

It's important to acknowledge that parenting can be stressful, and there may be times when you feel overwhelmed or unsure about how to handle a situation. That's when having a supportive team in place can make all the difference. Whether it's your partner, family members, or friends, having people you can rely on for emotional support, advice, and assistance can help make the transition into parenthood smoother and more manageable.

Effective teamwork involves good communication, mutual respect, and a willingness to share responsibilities. Talk to your partner or support system about your expectations and work together to create a plan for caring for your baby. Remember that each person brings their own strengths and weaknesses to the table, so it's important to be flexible and open-minded. By working as a team, you can provide the best possible care for your baby and create a supportive environment for everyone involved. Remember, you've got this, mama!

Even if you and your partner have a good working together relationship, just being a new parent can be a stressful situation. It is essential to prioritize self-care and practice mindfulness to maintain physical and emotional well-being. Support from family and friends or a therapist can be very helpful during this period. Self-care is not selfish, and moms should take advantage of any downtime to take care of themselves. It is a lifestyle change that can avoid stress and depression.

There are many ways to take care of yourself, such as taking a nap, relaxing in a bath, going for a walk, doing yoga, reading a book, writing in a journal, or getting a massage. A date night with your partner or friends is also highly recommended for new parents to connect with each other. Being mindful of your mental health will ensure a smooth transition into parenthood for you, your partner, and your baby.

Postpartum depression, anxiety, and other mental health concerns are not uncommon among new parents, and they can have a significant impact on a person's well-being. It's important to recognize the signs of these conditions and to seek help as soon as possible. This might involve talking to a healthcare provider, a mental health professional, or joining a support group. Seeking help is not a sign of weakness but rather a proactive step towards maintaining good mental health.

In addition to mental health concerns, new parents may also experience other complications such as breastfeeding difficulties, sleep deprivation, or healing from a c-section. Seeking professional help for these issues can make a significant difference in a person's recovery and overall well-being. A lactation consultant can help new parents navigate breastfeeding challenges, while a physical therapist can provide guidance on postpartum exercise and recovery. Don't feel embarrassed to seek professional help. The faster you feel like your old self, the better the motherhood journey will be.

Research has shown that being a parent can release endorphins, resulting in high levels of feel-good hormones like oxytocin. After becoming a new mom, you will fully understand that a newborn requires patience, compassion, and unconditional love, and while it can be challenging, the joy of watching a tiny life grow makes it all worthwhile. But you will also learn that newborns can really test you and put you under a lot of stress with all the crying.

Remember, newborns communicate through crying as their only way of expressing their needs, wants, and feelings. In the first month, babies can cry for up to three hours per day, which can be overwhelming for new parents. Hunger is the main reason why newborns cry, as they have small stomachs and need to feed more often than older children and adults. Cluster feedings, nursing frequently in a short period, are an important part of newborn care, providing essential nutrients for growth and development.

Understanding why newborns cry, knowing how to meet their needs, and recognizing when they are overstimulated or in pain can help new parents navigate the first month of their baby's life. Again, as a reminder, if the crying is triggering you, seek help or put the baby in a safe space while you step away for a few minutes to clear your mind and gather your thoughts.

It's okay to get overwhelmed yourself, mama. There is no shame in that. As you navigate this new motherhood journey, you will learn things along the way. No two moms experience the same situations, and all babies are different. I wrote this book to help point you in the right direction of some basic things you can expect when it comes to taking care of a newborn, but you might also have unique experiences, and that is normal.

While books on newborn care can be incredibly helpful, it's essential to remain flexible and adaptable as you care for your specific baby's needs. Just like adults, babies have different personalities, preferences, and needs, and it's essential to recognize and respect these differences.

For example, while some babies may be content to sleep for long stretches at night, others may wake frequently to eat or need more help falling asleep. Some babies may prefer a certain type of pacifier or bottle, while others may not take to it at all. It's important to remain open to trying different things and finding what works best for your specific baby.

It's also important to remember that babies develop at their own pace. While books on newborn care can provide helpful guidelines on what to expect in terms of developmental milestones, every baby will reach these milestones in their own time. In the newborn stage, some babies may lift their heads sooner or track objects sooner than others, and that's okay.

However, staying on top of monitoring developmental milestones in newborns is an essential aspect of identifying any delays or difficulties in their intellectual, emotional, and physical development. These milestones also help doctors determine whether the infant has any underlying health problems related to development. Keeping track of developmental advances is important to ensure a baby's well-being and build the foundation to carry them into successful childhood years.

By acknowledging that every baby is different, new parents can approach their role with greater flexibility, patience, and understanding. Rather than getting caught up in comparison or frustration when things don't go as expected, parents can remain open to learning and growing alongside their baby. Ultimately, the more attuned parents are to their baby's unique needs and preferences, the better they will be able to provide the care and support their baby needs to thrive.

During the first few months of life, babies reach many developmental milestones. They develop the ability to recognize familiar voices and respond with facial expressions, sharpen their senses, and gain head control. It's essential to engage in activities such as reading, singing, and talking to encourage healthy development, identify any developmental delays or health concerns early on, and establish a strong parent-child relationship. As babies grow, age-appropriate activities such as playing music, dancing, and mirror play can have significant benefits. Playing music can help babies develop sensory perception, language processing, and memory formation, while dancing can promote physical, social, and emotional development. Mirror play can help babies recognize themselves, develop visual recognition and fine motor skills, and encourage speech-language development.

So why not try some of these fun activities with your little one and watch them thrive?

Being a new mom can be exhausting and overwhelming, but the good news is that the newborn stage only lasts for three months. At this point, babies start gaining control of their head movements, respond actively to stimuli, and demonstrate increased coordination. Caregivers should start introducing activity-based learning experiences to help the baby's brain development and emotional well-being.

Another important aspect of parenting is to ==trust your instincts.== You may not have all the answers or the experience, but you know your baby better than anyone else. No one knows your baby better than you do, and you will learn to read their cues and needs over time. Don't be afraid to try different approaches and methods, and find what works best for you and your baby.

Remember that parenting is a journey, and there will be ups and downs along the way. It is important to celebrate the small victories and milestones and not be too hard on yourself when things don't go as planned. Babies are unpredictable, and it's normal to make mistakes. Learn from them, and keep moving forward.

Finally, enjoy the journey. Parenthood can be challenging, but it is also a beautiful and rewarding experience. Take the time to cherish the moments with your baby, and remember that they grow up fast. The sleepless nights and endless diaper changes may seem never-ending, but soon you will look back on this time with nostalgia and fondness.

In conclusion, parenting is an incredible journey that can be overwhelming at times, but with the right support, self-care, and a positive attitude, you can navigate through it successfully. Don't hesitate to ask for help or advice from family, friends, or healthcare professionals. They are there to support you and provide you with guidance. You've got this, and congratulations on becoming a parent!

If you've found this book helpful, please don't forget to leave a review on Amazon. Your review can truly help another mom trying to narrow down which book to buy, and it also shows your support toward the author.
Thank you for choosing "Newborn Care Made Easy."

Checklist - Newborn Essentials
Clothing Items

- Onesies
    - 5 onesies in newborn size
    - 10 onesies in 0-3 months size
- Long Sleeve Bodysuit
    - Fall/Winter Baby
        - 5 in newborn size
        - 10 in 0-3 months size
    - Spring/Summer Baby
        - 3 in newborn size
        - 5 in 0-3 months
- Pants
    - 3 pants in newborn size
    - pants in 0-3 months size
- Footie Pajamas
    - 5 in newborn size
    - 10 in 0-3 months size
    - Note: I think the footie PJs were the easiest to work with in the newborn stages. Also, as a pro tip, avoid the snap-up style and just go with the zip-up kind.

- Hats and Mittens
    - 3 Hats
    - 5 Mittens
- Socks
    - 12 pairs of 0-3 months
- Outerwear
    - Fall/Winter Baby
        - 1 Coat or bunting outfit
        - 2 Sweaters or Hoodies
- Swaddles
    - 3-4 Swaddles
- Blankets
    - 2 Baby blankets

Checklist - Feeding Essentials
Breastfeeding

- Breast pump (many are covered by insurance, so don't forget to check)
- Breast pump parts
- Breast milk storage bags
- Nipple Cream
- Nursing Bras
- Nursing Pads
- Baby bottles
- Slow-flow nipples for the bottles
- Burb cloths
- Bottlebrush

Checklist - Feeding Essentials
Formula Feeding

- Formula
- Baby bottles
- Slow flow nipples
- Bottle warmer
- Burp cloths
- Bottlebrush

Checklist - Newborn Essentials
Must Have Items

- Carseat
- Stroller
- Diapers
- Diaper rash cream
- Diaper bag
- Baby bathing supply
    - Baby body wash
    - Baby shampoo
    - Baby washcloths
    - Baby towels
- Sick Baby Supplies
    - Rectal Thermometer
    - Infant Pain Reliever
    - Snot Sucker / Nasal Aspirator
    - Humidifier
    - Saline Spray
    - Petroleum Jelly
    - Pedialyte

- Baby Monitor
- Baby Swing
- Pacifier
- Teethers
- Electric Nail Trimmer

Checklist - Newborn Items
Nice to Haves

- Baby rockers and bouncers
- Wipes warmers
- Bottle washers
- Sterilizers
- Diaper pail
- Wearable baby carrier
- Stroller accessories
- Wipes warmer
- Bottle sterilizer
- Baby toys
- Activity Mat
- Jumpers
- Bath accessories
- Sound machine
- Rocking chair

Checklist - Hospital Bag
Hospital Bag Checklist

- Snack Ideas to Pack
    - Trail mix
    - Granola bars
    - Your favorite chips
    - Pretzels
    - Bananas
    - Peanut butter
    - Dark chocolate
    - Yogurt
    - Pudding cups
    - Muffins
    - Beef jerky
    - Dates
    - Baby carrots
    - Almonds
    - Electrolyte drinks - Gatorade or coconut water

- Toiletries
    - Hairbrush
    - Toothbrush & toothpaste
    - Deodorant
    - Chapstick
    - Hair ties
    - Face wipes
    - Shampoo
    - Body wash
    - Lotion
- Entertainment
    - Books
    - Tablet
    - Chargers
- Comfy Clothing
    - Comfortable robe
    - Pajamas
    - Slippers
    - Cozy grip socks
    - Going home outfit
    - Granny panties
    - Nursing bras

- Postpartum Products
    - Peri Bottle
    - Maxi Pads
    - Witch Hazel Pads
    - Perineal Spray
    - Miralax
    - Nipple Cream
- Packing Items for the Baby
    - Going home outfit for baby
    - Onesies
    - A small pack of diapers/wipes
    - Receiving blanket
    - Swaddles
    - Baby bottle (optional)
    - Car seat - have your car seat properly installed before going to the hospital.

Other Mamas' Said....

Amanda:
There are alternatives for petroleum jelly. If you are trying to find more organic solutions try shea butter or jojoba oil. Also if you are planning to use cloth diapers, there are adjustable ones with snaps to fit a variety of sizes that you can also use with liners to make poop cleanup easier.

Krista C:
Co-sleeping with a newborn is not common, but some mom's choose to co-sleep. It is important to know that it can be done, but it's also essential that it is done properly because it can be dangerous. It's recommended to follow the Safe Sleep 7 guidelines.

Grace:
As a new mom one pro tip, is don't forget to eat. Keep healthy snacks on hand and drink plenty of water as this can help with keeping your breastmilk supply up. Also, when it comes to bathing the baby, you don't only have to give them a bath, showering with a newborn is also an option.

Samantha:
Don't forget that you can hire a doula!

Other Mamas' Said....

Tana:

After delivering a baby, it's important to remember that it can take a few days for your milk to come in. If you plan to breastfeed, it's recommended to explore different feeding positions to find the one that suits your baby's preference and your own comfort. Additionally, introducing bottle feeding alongside breastfeeding is perfectly fine. To avoid bottle rejection, I suggest introducing a bottle between 4-6 weeks of age and practicing with it.

If you're a busy mom who is always on the go, investing in a few baby carriers can be a great idea. As a mom of multiple children, I personally find it convenient to use a sling ring carrier while I chase after my toddler. It allows me to easily feed and nap the newborn while on the move.

Kathy:

While you are busy baby proofing your nursey, consider the future too. Once your child starts crawling, walking, and climbing there are many other things they can get into. Put effort into locking up drawers and making a habit of keeping things like pills, essential oils, and CBD gummies in a safe place.

References

0-1 month: newborn development. (2023, February 21). Raising Children Network. https://raisingchildren.net.au/newborns/development/development-tracker/0-1-month

Asmundsson, L. (2022). A Week-by-Week Guide to Your Baby's First Year Milestones. *Parents.* https://www.parents.com/baby/development/growth/baby-development-week-by-week/

Developmental milestones for baby. (n.d.). March of Dimes. https://www.marchofdimes.org/find-support/topics/parenthood/developmental-milestones-baby

Earley, B., & Earley, B. (2022). Best Activities for a Newborn. *What to Expect.* https://www.whattoexpect.com/playroom/playtime-tips/maximizing-baby-alert-time.aspx

Pampers. (2022). Activities to Do With Your Newborn. *Web-Pampers-US-EN.* https://www.pampers.com/en-us/baby/activities/article/newborn-activities

References

What is a Developmental Milestone? (2022, December 29). Centers for Disease Control and Prevention. https://www.cdc.gov/ncbddd/actearly/milestones/index.html

Made in the USA
Columbia, SC
27 December 2024